Awaken

The Definitive Guide to
Transformative
Change

Robyn G. Locke

GIVEN BY THE ELDERS

Awaken: The Definitive Guide to Transformative Change
Published by Golden Page Publishing
Atlanta, GA

ISBN: 978-0-9992458-7-3 (Amazon)
ISBN: 978-8-9877542-0-7 (Ingram)

Library of Congress Control Number: 2022947443
BODY, MIND & SPIRIT / Healing / Energy

QUANTITY PURCHASES: Schools, companies, professional groups, clubs, and other organizations may qualify for special terms when ordering quantities of this title. Email info@AdvancedEnergetics.org for more details.

Table of Contents

In Appreciation

My unconditional love is given to the Elders, who have infused me with a renewed understanding of all that is. Their insights provide the intrinsic components I've yearned to discover.

A heart-felt thanks is extended to Diane who guided me through the past life regression shared here from the Elders' vantage. To Janet and Suzanne for their ongoing support. And to Lorna, Lorie, Victoria, Andrea, and Polly who enabled what is before you to be made tangible and real.

I hope you, too, locate some noteworthy revelations as you embark on your own personal journey to heal, restore and renew.

Introduction

U niversal law enables activities and initiatives to seamlessly and rapidly fall into place when you are moving within its flow. When you are in step with the flow of consciousness, moving in this manner allows you to resonate with Universal Source. Outside of this flow, seeming stagnation and resistance are often the results you encounter. You know this to be true when your actions appear restricted and making progress seems to be oh-so-difficult. When you are outside of the flow of life, you have stepped onto land and are no longer moving with the swiftness of the water's current. Yet while you are in the current, you will more surely race in the direction that the flow will take you. Maybe not where you thought you would go, but where you are now directed.

Do you know or wonder about your purpose? Do you know what it is? Do you seek wholeness to develop, create, give service, or simply want to have happier thoughts? Is it possible to retrain the mind so that it does not continually repeat itself in reminding you of some misstep from past times but rather to focus on better or happier things?

And what steps can you take to begin to uncover what has accumulated in your body due to your past choices? We are not talking about dietary choices, although those decisions can also weigh heavily on the body. We are talking about those emotions which you have chosen not to feel. Instead, because you have not fully embraced them, they have been internalized and stored. Each has been placed within your body for you to access and feel later.

Every one of those unfelt emotions is ever so securely kept safe for you within your body. They are there for your later use. Surely you will want to feel them since that is why you sought to incarnate here. To feel and experience life on this planet. So the energy of each emotion is kept safe and secure until you seek a connection with them. In time, you may have other similar unexpressed feelings that are stored with the original one. All will be kept together for the time when you are ready to engage them. Then, through your engagement, you will allow their energy to be released in feeling and by associating with these emotions.

How and where are these emotions kept within your body? How can you sleuth out such details? And is there a quick process to activate their release? Yes, these will be discussed along with an overview to better understand stored energy. This energy can also be referred to as trapped emotions. In time, this energy develops a life of its own. They out-picture themselves in ways not fully anticipated. Are you aware of this occurrence? A foundational understanding will be provided so all trapped energy can be released before they fester.

This self-discovery work will set the platform and serve as a springboard to the next step. For the initial steps are necessary to bring you to a greater understanding of the tools that you can lay claim to soon.

Our long-held desire is to share various healing modalities. Yet, first, you must have a rudimentary idea of what you may have already created within. We seek to get you to a place of centeredness so that you can take command and control of your life. And in that better space, use the new tools to remove obstacles from your body and live the life of your intentions. Most certainly, these pages will allow changes to occur in your life. To return your focus to bringing forward your heart's desire, your true purpose.

Health and healing are necessary ingredients to ensure a happy future. When you are reminded of some healing modalities that were available to you in other times, certainly you will want to immediately implement them. Can you now see that there is something more expansive in store for your future after you make a few tweaks or adjustments necessitated by previous life choices?

And Love. How does Love enter into the equation? Love is a word that has come to mean an emotion towards oneself, another, an object, but something that is understood in a defined way. It becomes somewhat limited in this perfectly defined understanding. In that limited understanding, it does not allow for the expansiveness Love does surely encompass. Love is so much more than described by its more routinely used definition. It is so much more.

Know that Love is truly an underlying component within all of life. Attune to the depths that Love does allow as it shifts you and offers new levels of healing. It does allow for different outcomes to be experienced. There is a unique vibrational quality to what we will call Universal Love. This is an expansive Love that will be more fully discussed in coming pages. Know that once activated within your world, this Love will shift those things it engages with — allowing for so much more to be.

There are many such things that have lost their full potency and measure as time has advanced. We do hope to revisit and reintroduce more in time. For it is a remembering of sorts. Once re-engaged, more opportunities will be open to you. Allow for that which was, and is, to again be understood and realized. Do so while you are in your current form as you live in this world of form.

Do integrate with this work and perhaps feel your way. Know that as you merge with your thoughts, you do become a part of them. You create a bridge to allow your thoughts to become one and a part of you. That is so in this work. In doing so, you will expand your awareness. Just as you focus intently on your profession or hobby, devote time to this endeavor. In this way, you can move beyond current limitations and become a more expansive you.

This is key in accomplishing the upcoming steps. For each step is a building block to the next. And so, as you incorporate one understanding, you do grow into the next. So collectively, the full measure of what we seek to impart can be experienced, felt, and known. And you will become the limitless creator of all you want to accomplish in this lifetime and so much more.

How to Receive to Perceive

Do you see that all is possible when you begin from the heart space? Begin in that way each time you read here. Ask for clarity and understanding. Set the intention that more is to be. Set the intention to read with your heart as opposed to your head. Seek and ye shall find. Move in an unbridled way. Each time you stop or pause reading, begin again by focusing on your heart and asking for more to be. Ask for more to be understood, and that you move always in the clarity of Love.

When you see this symbol, practice and
play with the exercises given.

In this way, you will enact a different tomorrow
having planted their seeds this day.

Given by the Elders

Chapter 1

Where We Began and Now Do Begin

Trust and Believe

When you give into trust, you tell Universe you believe in the beauty and possibilities It might impart. This is an acceptance of sorts of what might be, could be, within your being and world. This is the greatest indicator that you are ready to relinquish the controls of life to Universe and Universal knowing. Then, the manifestation process can be stepped up, and so much more can potentially be given. Do you see this?

We seek, as does Universe, to show you the endless potential of the expansive opportunities that await all you desire to create. It seems there are often unnecessary restrictions placed upon lives through the mind and choices made, rather than allowing what might otherwise be made manifest. We suggest you seek no limitation or restriction, which would slow Universal flow.

Think upon comments made to friends when such things are not believed. Can you recall times when you provided an answer to another person with a contrived response, not fully connected or aligned with your core beliefs? Or do you enter into an activity where you share more freely than when operating outside of it? Perhaps you have lessened your resistance from time to time and have shared openly what is believed at your core. Do you understand what is meant here? How often do you respond affirmatively while actually believing conversely? During such conversations, do you engage in positive, uplifted dialog of how to achieve a successful outcome? Or, rather than positive points, did negative dialog enter in to offset what was desired? In other words, do the negative what ifs of life become a central focus and shift your contemplated objectives?

And when you are in a more fluid state, not having fully anchored within what is wanted, do desired objectives seem achievable or not so much? Know your core beliefs must be ferreted out. If you do not hold them as you would a deeply felt conviction but only offer lip service, then you will find it more challenging to engage or enlist the full return of what we seek to impart here.

And what about soul fragmentation? Are you aware of this possibility, as many have discussed it? If not, consider how the Soul seeks to minimize Its losses. Now might you further consider this expanded understanding?

Soul Fragmentation: Recognize this can occur when a Soul experiences something unexpected, exists in a manner that is less than, or is engaged from a perspective of lack. Here, there is the ability for the Soul to pull away from what is. In a manner of speaking, it is a lessening of the tethering aspect that is then in play.

And so when one is tethered to something considered to be of a lesser nature, then the Soul releases a portion of Itself so that more does not remain attached to that lesser state. There is an acknowledging that in time, an energetic reformulation will need to take place. And this energetic aspect will need to be revisited so that a reintegration might occur. In many ways, there is a lessening of the loss experienced then. For were the Soul to remain more fully engaged and not fragment in this way — more loss might occur. And so, it is, in essence, cutting Its losses during this fragmentation process.

If a traumatic occurrence is underway, the Soul Essence experiences more of a shattering effect. Although soul fragmentation may result here, there is also the possibility for an energetic matrix to be created. Often, these exist simultaneously and come into play in this way.

Over time, the Soul will desire to reintegrate that which had become fractured, less than, and incomplete. A means of restoration will exist throughout the Soul's subsequent incarnations to integrate or reintegrate aspects and become whole once again.

Often, the Soul remains, to some degree, aware of the occurrence. As you might suspect, were the Soul to simply remove Itself, the body vessel would not be able to fully function. And so, when there is the fragmentation aspect, a limited amount of Spiritual Essence remains to stay engaged with what is occurring so a more immediate death does not result.

Yet there is another component to be considered as we set the stage for our backstory. An earlier incarnation of the one who hears our communications, and has crafted this book, is shared for you now to know a little of her story. In that way, we may all proceed together at the same level of understanding. We add here some points for clarity.

In an earlier time, this one did make a life-changing discovery which, in many ways, defined her future. And so consider when a life-shattering occurrence is experienced, do you yet understand the value of such a thing? Why it arrived and what you might recognize from it? Might you value it as being a messenger of what it sought to impart? Did you ever realize that even those things which appear to be bad are actually sent to you as a means of direction as you contemplate your next step? Might we suggest the perspective taken by the one whose path it has crossed is the next most critical step? For you see, so many things are dependent upon how you interpret them.

And so in working with the energy in play, some Souls have carried an unexpressed burden with them from another time. We do not discuss what some believe to be the purpose of reincarnation, but rather an energetic matrix created when death occurs from a deep-seated grief or psychological trauma. When an unexpected situation shatters and disrupts a life, there may not be the time, nor the inclination, to feel the experience. So the personality quickly retreats from life and often dies. By personality, we mean to discuss the one who acts out the life experience. Different personalities of the same Soul act out varied life experiences through various incarnations.

Although an untimely death is often the result, there is also a residual aspect that maintains an energetic, connective frequency. This aspect can continue beyond the personality's death. And so, there is a photographic imprint of sorts that maintains an energetic projection for an unspecified amount of time, if not indefinitely. Sometimes these are felt as energetic disturbances. Know these energy hiccups can also create a unique energetic field. This imprint exists in relation to and beyond the personality who, many times, unknowingly created it. Although soul fragmentation may result, an energetic imprint might also occur.

You see, when the personality utilized a limited perspective in their interpretation of an experience that resulted in a dramatic or oftentimes traumatic shift, the resulting limitation (in some ways) continues to be imprinted within the future incarnations connected with this Soul Essence. Many times such a situation does result in death. The imprint does not exist as karma might suggest, but rather, it exists so that whatever is not complete might become whole once again. So whatever component was lacking, this might become a part of the lens used to mete out future dealings or objectives.

This situation sometimes results in a behind-the-scenes mission, so to speak, as the Essence seeks to assimilate and resolve what occurred in the lifetime when the energetic scar was created. When the assimilation ultimately occurs, a resolution results and the energetic imbalance is released. You see, when the criteria is resolved, clarity results as a greater understanding is imparted when such a connection is made. Balance is restored. For this lifestream, it was the need to discern more keenly. And so, for many lifetimes, discernment issues arose, and that issue remained active until most recently when a reconnection took place between two lifetimes by two personalities of the same Soul.

Shortcomings created by an untimely death were resolved when an assimilation occurred in this lifetime. Small portions of the originating past life story were recalled and are given here to more vividly convey what was experienced both then and now.

You see, because we have an energetic tie to this one who communicates our words, we seek for you to know her a bit better in the process. And so know as she is grateful for our words, we, too, are grateful for her diligence to these writings as a small portion of her past is shared with you now.

A child who was merely thirteen went to study the occult

in another land, long ago. She traveled away from family and friends to live out her life in further study with others who also sought to understand and expand their psychic gifts. There was a great joy of being a part of a group of women who worked at such an endeavor. Their work was seen as an honor and an enterprise that was highly regarded.

She had gone there to learn how to bridge the physical with the nonphysical world. In her daily activities, she knew many of us who work with and through her today. We observed her and the energy she emanated then, for she was full of hope and promise. She leapt to each activity and carried out her objectives with such joy and loving ambition. By ambition, we mean to say how joyously she looked upon each undertaking as she did so with unyielding passion and unwavering devotion.

In time, she introduced and made many other announcements for some of the oracles. By oracles, we mean those who were gifted with the ability to profess future occurrences, readings, and other spiritual gifts. They shared their insights with those who sought such knowledge. Routinely, many of the townspeople would gather to hear messages imparted by these gifted ones as they also financially supported them.

So at nineteen years of age, after having studied for many years, she made a discovery during one of her many introductory remarks. That morning as she made one such introduction, she pieced together and became aware of certain missing components as she spoke to the crowd. She realized inaccuracies of those she had introduced and the incongruences that existed there. She suddenly realized a basic premise was missing from some whom she had supported and were void of the truths she thought their words had reflected. This new awareness cut through her like a knife. Her strong beliefs were shattered. Her trust dashed. It was for her a mortal wound from which she could not, would not recover. It took her breath away. She could no longer speak as before. She now spoke in but a hushed whisper.

She did not re-enter the temple walls but sat along the roadside, ashamed and aghast she had not seen what was so plainly visible to her now. Not all were dishonest. Only a few there were untrustworthy. But not knowing whom to trust, she chose to trust no one. She no longer engaged with any who had acted as her family for those many years. It left her with an empty feeling inside and caused her to question all she had come to believe in and trust. This was a most devastating blow for her to experience and one that was totally unexpected. She has carried that burden with her in each subsequent lifetime, in some form or fashion.

Along with enlisting trust and belief, discernment is also a critical component. You must look, listen, and discover what it means to discern. Discernment can impact all aspects of your life. You see, you cannot listen to every individual and give them the same standing as you might bestow upon a trusted family member or close friend. You must trust your intuition or gut to know if these individuals are seeking to enlighten or rob you of your time and money. Discernment is key in all of your daily dealings and in your spiritual life too. Guard to protect what you believe to be truthful and then verify to confirm your beliefs inwardly.

This story did not have a happy ending until most recently. In revisiting that lifetime, there was an opportunity to impart something of value to the child who was so grief-stricken that she no longer saw purpose in living. She felt she had, although unknowingly, deceived many within her community.

So, most recently, there was an energetic connection made, and a release occurred between these two personalities residing in two different times. The release took place when there was a preference (in this lifetime) to connect to the grief, connect to this teenage personality, and provide her with comfort and love. There was an insistence to give love to this shattered one who lay curled up against a wall on the roadside. You see, the former personality was distraught with grief and still energetically out-pictured that anguish, although not on the physical plane.

When the current connection was made to give this one comfort and love, the cycle stopped, and the release occurred. It was a most reverent thing to witness. It was a most holy act when one aspect connected to another aspect of self. Time was bridged to allow both personalities to embrace. Comfort and love were given to this child. So the release was quickly experienced. It was fully felt as if no gap in time existed. It was a most seamless occurrence. For truly there is no time or space in the Nowness of It. All is occurring in a most congruent manner.

Trust and belief can now be experienced more readily by this one who has pushed through these same issues in her present life. Always second-guessing and doubting what would more readily come to be recognized and accepted by another. This was a momentous occurrence as it allowed for a release and a shift to take place. As each personality came together to bridge time and space, assimilations restored the wholeness which had been sought.

You see, you need not experience any past life, especially to revisit one that led to such an abrupt end. When you encounter any unresolved issue, whatever it might be, just surrender it. In that recognition, you can release what no longer serves you. Meditate, or choose another way to determine any limitations that exist for you in your surrender of them. Then you can move forward by leaving those things on the table, so to speak, as you embrace all in Love. With Love, transmutation can occur, and you can reclaim precious aspects lost in another time.

Again we will say to trust only self. Allow others to provide you with insights and new understandings, but then do the work to confirm their words. Always move within for inner counsel and direction. Moving forward, seek to know when words are given for your advancement or for another's self-aggrandizement. See how this resonates with you now as you trust and believe with discernment.

We share this story so you might embark upon some noteworthy discoveries of your own. This book will elicit more personal revelations and realizations to occur as your hidden treasures resurface, as internal tools are recognized, as illness and disease are minimized, and as you embark on a journey that will demystify your purpose or reason for living in the Nowness of this time. Allow for all you desire to become visible as you champion all you seek to accomplish in this life.

You see, each step has led you here, and this step propels your next one. Your journey begins anew as you explore the coming pages that will have you participate in a bit of your own journey of self-discovery.

So know each choice is worthwhile, and each direction will shift your reality to yet another series of choices. Relinquish what is unnecessary and lighten the energetic load as you unknowingly carry these things. New choices abound as you turn the page, and this process begins anew as it unfolds unique unto you.

Chapter 2

Be in the Flow

How often do you say or feel things aren't going your way? During special occasions or over the holidays, how and with whom do you spend them? Conflict seems to enter into the mix when time has to be divided between family and other social obligations. It may be difficult to enjoy special celebrations if they are coupled with the anniversary of something you would rather not remember. Festivities can heighten your senses when expectations raise your anticipation of what was, might be, could have been, or what might be termed as the *what ifs* of life.

Do you feel obligated during the holidays to get with family members when you would just rather hang out with friends? How can you set into motion some new routines, and why does that seem so difficult to do? It sometimes seems like you want anything except what you already have, or does it just feel that way? Does the mind create a longing in opposition to what exists? So what is working against you to take that next step?

Ego is usually the culprit. It shifts you away from those things you might otherwise enjoy. Ego seems to want what is not readily available, what is not occurring in your present moment. A part of its original design was meant to protect its host during a fight or flight period during mankind's early evolution. But that role is no longer needed. The saber-toothed feline is extinct and won't be blocking your path anytime soon.

Perhaps ego's mission has morphed a bit, for the opposition we describe seems to lie within. This is the ego of today as it tries to maintain relevance by engaging the mind in the what ifs of life and in its oppositional thinking.

In many scenarios, ego reasserts its significance by taking the opposing side of a storyline. If you say something is black or white, well, ego might tell you how it is gray. How else might it try to justify its existence? But we share how the majority of what it protects is not you. In many individuals, it creates depression, anger and despondency, while keeping happier thoughts at bay.

Why is this? How often do you hear a nagging voice in your head that seems to take a perfectly normal and otherwise beautiful day and drag it down a notch or two by engaging in negative mental chatter? Universal law enters into the equation by gathering more of the energy you are engaged with to return more of it back to you. The vibration will go out, gather more of its kind, so you have an even greater abundance of it. You are sent more of the vibrational match, of what you seemingly want more of, through your focused attention. More of what Source, Universe or however you define this Omnipotent Power, believes you want. This would further compound a not so good situation if you are thinking unhappy thoughts, right? Do you see why awareness is so necessary and why refocusing negative inner dialogs to happier ones is key as you go about your day? When you think good thoughts and those thoughts gather more of their kind, you are able to maintain better thoughts more easily. You enable more of their vibrational kind to flow back to you.

As you go about your afternoon, isn't it better to drive around with a smile on your face? To recognize the uniqueness of being so happy as you chuckle while simply enjoying the prosperity of life today? We say unique, as is this the way you normally see things? Can you see this? When you met up with a friend to enjoy a nice lunch at a local restaurant, can you appreciate this simple experience? Will you engage with the sheer happiness of the moment and be present in it? Welcome those things you enjoy, rather than dwelling on thoughts that make you feel unhappy. You want more of what makes you feel good, right? You see, when conversations meld together with your thoughts, more of those are gathered and returned to you. In that state of contentedness, you re-engage with other similar thoughts, and this results in experiencing a better day.

Are you consciously aware that thoughts run almost nonstop in your mind throughout the day? Do you allow whatever floats in there to remain your main focus for an unlimited amount of time? Do you believe you are creating these thoughts? Can you see again that ego is the culprit? Do you understand why it makes sense for you to become aware of what is playing in the background of your mind, the role of your subconscious, and the need to remain present along the way? Your thoughts impact your life and how you handle things. These thoughts affect your day. And you most surely will move throughout your day differently if you are focused on more uplifting, happier things.

It is sometimes difficult to maintain good thoughts, but can some-thing be added here? If we were to take this one concept a step further, how might such thinking affect your body? Consider your thoughts and recognize the vibration and resonance created by them. So if your body is a receptacle and repository for the energy you create, how does that work?

You see your body stores many things for your intended use. Since all is energetic in nature, might you recognize that finding space within is not the issue? It's so handy to locate things such as emotional energy in the body as it is readily accessible for you to find, focus, and feel.

So think about your body now and the stresses and concerns which are placed upon it. And so, you might realize the mental ups and downs and the tremendous burden daily life might bestow. You know this after experiencing the mental consequences resulting from such things as stress, depression, anxiety, and general unhappiness. These things are sometimes out-pictured by high blood pressure, chronic headaches, and the like. But what if you were to make efforts to keep your body and mind in a more even keel? Guard and monitor what you maintain your focus upon and shift from unhappy thoughts, when they are recognized, to happier ones. What then?

You have probably heard of positive thinking and its attributes. And you can easily rationalize that maintaining better thoughts should make you feel happier. Suffice it to say this is of the utmost importance. Know and seek to remain consciously aware of what you are thinking. Maintain present moment awareness. Strive to remain in this state of awareness as you continually adjust your focus to those thoughts which make you feel better.

**THOUGHTS CAN RUN RAMPANT
UNLESS YOU BEGIN TO MONITOR THEM
AND BECOME AWARE OF WHAT IS PLAYING
IN THE BACKGROUND OF YOUR MIND**

YOU ARE NOT YOUR THOUGHTS

What you focus upon goes out energetically, gathers more of its kind before coming back to you. Your energy will always return full circle since you are its energetic creator. It's an incredible thing to know your focus can provide you with more of anything. Do you see how you can create more of what you want each day, in large part, when you maintain or shift into desired thoughts? When you focus your mind on things you want, you attract them into your life. Soon you will see the benefits positive thoughts will bring to your day. As you do this work, would you rather receive more of something you enjoy, like those things which make you feel good? You certainly don't want to bring more depressing thoughts or activities to your doorstep. You see, it is really that simple. What you seek is what you will find, time and time again.

So your body works to support those thoughts and beliefs you focus upon. Likewise, your body maintains much within the day without too much notice or direction. All the goings-on there and how so much is accomplished from blood flow, digestion to body regulation. Well, it's nothing short of miraculous. Do you agree? Do you ever wonder how this happens? How is it possible for so much to take place without you providing oversight or giving implicit instruction? Think of it. You manage your life and the lives of many others, either directly or indirectly. But how does your body perform so effortlessly without your continual input? How does it accomplish so much without more direction and interjection from you?

It is worth discussing here because there are things that influence how your body works and where the breakdowns occur. Do you wonder how an ache or two developed in your back or shoulders when you did nothing notable to irritate them? Why cancer cells accelerate and how high blood pressure develops?

Pain is an indicator alerting you that something is off. So you enlist the advice of doctors. Do you take one doctor's opinion or get several opinions? Sometimes, the diagnosis is obvious, but other times only a best guess can be given — one that is based on the expertise and knowledge of your physician and their colleagues.

So it is during this time that you analyze what you have or have not done within your life. These are the things that have gotten you to where you are today. Do you see them as indicators on your path of what you have previously thought, said, or done? They all bring you to where you reside this day. Nothing is wrong with that, and in fact, each step you have taken is a very good thing. You are where you are meant to be … where life has brought you through a series of choices which were designed to keep you moving forward in the direction of your intent.

Also consider how you brought a unique intention with you as you entered this lifetime. Yes, you do have a reason for being that only you can vibrationally bring forth. You are the sole actor on the stage of life who can provide the gifts you seek to manifest here. You see, you are your unique gifts. And if not you, who else will be able to bring them into manifestation? You are it. Only you can bring these things into the world as you would, as you will.

Do you understand this concept? Who else can bring your special gifts into manifestation, if not you? If you do not do so, will they ever be? And do you realize when things align for you to bring your gifts into being, this itself is a miraculous thing? It is incredible when all aspects converge for this creation to come into existence.

We do so want to impart the significance of being in Universal flow within this time. This is how you can more easily manifest what you sought to create. Being in its flow will also allow those things lodged within to be revealed in a more seamless and amazingly simple manner. When you are in Universal flow, you will accomplish your objectives in an effortless way. Much more is enabled without forcing the situation or fighting against opposing energy. This is how it goes and how you will know if you are in or out of alignment with Universal Source.

So how do you get into Universal flow? First, stay within the realm of possibility as you focus upon a deeply held desire. There are those who believe they are to create something grand and perhaps even life-changing. Although this may be so, can you recall what you focused upon in earlier times? What did you want to grow up to become, do or be? Did you recognize any similarities in the roles you chose in your youth? Do reflect back to when you were a youngster and more carefree — before life's limitations were imposed upon you.

Where did you find your joy? What made you happy to think about doing then? Do you remember? If not, can you clear your mind in meditation? Meditate as you sit with the vastness of space that awaits your focus when your eyes are closed. Can you recite a mantra or words that have meaning to you, so the mental chatter stops for a brief time? And do you know the difference between the incessant mental dialog and the small voice within? Learn to recognize the distinction between the two and what this meek voice seeks to impart.

You see, you will know when you have encountered your dream, as it will resonate strongly with you and you with it. Do you know how to watch and be more attuned to this or how to make that awareness grow within you? By slowing the mind and looking within, you will find a greater understanding and know instinctively when you have hit upon it. There is a natural resonance that will emanate from you. As you become more conscious within your day, these indicators will further develop and grow to be more readily recognizable. You will know from internal indicators when you have finally connected with what you seek to discover. In this way you will more readily align with it.

But wait. Why is it not coming through yet? Why instead must you spend more time dealing with body ailments or aggravations that do not allow you to search for anything but relief from various aches and pains? Why does it all seem out of reach? And why do you feel less in tune with finding answers?

Being in Universal flow is where you want to be, but when you are outside of it — this is when you might seek to move back into the alignment such centeredness brings. Recognize and recall when you moved within its flow. Think back to when things occurred more seamlessly for you. Now, how might you return to that state of wonderment and being?

Chapter 3

How This Flows, Is How It Goes

Do you know the difference between when you accomplish something while in Universal flow and when you endeavor to achieve objectives outside of it? Returning into the flow is much easier when you can recognize and are consciously aware of having already operated within its dynamic portal of possibility and promise. Do you know the difference then? Is it readily apparent to you? Does, otherwise, swift movement feel more constrained or difficult to traverse when you are not in, what some know as the vortex? Does it sometimes seem as if you are pushing your way through life or forcing your will upon Universe?

Yet when you engage with life as you step into its flow, do you readily see the difference? Now when you move toward your destination, can you see the walkway shift to become a paved road as you jump into your car which will further accelerate your progress as you race onto the highway? Each will get you to your destination, but do you see the difference in speed and ease of travel when you are within its mighty dynamic current? Then you can seemingly arrive at where you want to be so much faster. You will attain anything you seek in less time, be less fatigued, and ready to take on your next adventure. Isn't that what you want from life? To discover what you want and be able to effortlessly accomplish more before discovering what you want next?

It is amazing when you are able to relinquish your tight hold on the various components held within this life. When you are able to get out of the way, you facilitate the flow. In this way, you permit its expansive energy to enter in. Thus innocent comments can remain as they were intended. Should you be subtly lectured, stop and deflect. When comments are taken personally, they can derail your day. Recognize those individuals who give instruction are merely instructing themselves. Give compassion and empathy to the one who is directing their energy at you. See this energy roll over, around, or pass through you.

The belief that somehow each conversation revolves around or relates to you, however, is one of the greatest obstructions to being in the flow. Do you think of another story to share rather than fully listening to their story? When a thought appears, and you latch onto it within the mind and marinate the concept with unending potency, do you later dwell in your thoughts and find a meaning you didn't initially think of earlier?

Perhaps a bad experience keeps playing in your mind. You keep reliving it. This energy remains in play and can further expand when it is engaged as gossip. This dynamic can grow the undesired energy when it is shared with others. Maybe you believe a different course of action would have resulted in a more preferred outcome. So in reliving a situation over and over again, you seek to revise it a bit and engage others so they might reinforce your perspective. This is of no real value. As you may know, each time you think about the occurrence, you re-engage with it. When you tell others about it, they expand the story's energetic dynamics. Those with whom you share your story form an opinion and engage it from their life experience, and then retell it to others. It's shared using a revised and exaggerated version of their own making.

Here you have taken something from the past and not left it there. It has been reintroduced into the present moment where it can be relived and multiplied when shared with others. Do you see how energetically it has become more anchored and in play now? This action may or may not even be what you believe to have happened. Well, it has created a life of its own by this storytelling. After all, currently, it is only a story. Can you say all components of this story are absolutely true? Or have certain details gotten twisted and turned it into an even more compelling drama?

Have you continually given these things renewed life by creating a more plausible, dramatic storyline? Do you go back and retell the story and restoke its embers, or do you allow others to keep the fire going? How might this be energetically reclaimed? When planting seeds, seek to nourish those that will sustain you. Weed out others that serve no lasting purpose. Reclaim the momentum established in earlier times, so your garden only grows things of value — those things that are vital and vibrant.

When a storyline is kept active, what then? Does the energy circle back to you as the originator of it? This has a multiplier effect, in that it is like the town crier of old. Energy, when introduced in such a fashion, does grow exponentially because so many do like to share stories. In the continual sharing of a story, the energy moves at a most staggering rate of speed. Surely some of the points or dynamics change when it is retold as exaggerations make it much more interesting and engaging. Thus it sometimes becomes larger than the actual life experience that occurred.

When your original story transitions into more of a group dynamic, then what? In this genre, there are competing storytellers who seek the most significant storyline. A group mentality of sorts is created here.

Within the group dynamic, there is a competition of sorts to be the best storyteller with the strongest storyline. Perhaps the desire here is to be the greatest sufferer. Victim attributes are big components found within such offerings as many seek to live their lives from a victim's role. What is unfortunate, besides what appears most apparent, is that often the victim does not have any other persona to move into should they seek to relinquish their victim-mentality status. So if the role of victim were to be relinquished, what other persona might be employed?

RELINQUISH THE STORY AND RECLAIM THE ENERGY FROM YOUR STORYTELLING

RELEASE THE DRAMA AS IT NO LONGER SERVES YOU

Let us look closer at this group dynamic and what happens when others recount your story. Oftentimes, those engaged here want to gain fellowship and friendship through an entertaining story. What isn't thought of at the time is how the story grows beyond the telling of it. Reclaim your energy. Reclaim the momentum and then follow the steps given to shift into a better space.

Perhaps, now too, consider the storyline of those who have advanced in age to continually recount stories of various aches and pains. As age advances, do spiritual objectives lessen? When self-identification reinforces body ailments, seek rather to align focus upon what might uplift. Association with undesired things will further anchor them in place. Seek rather to no longer tether these unwanted things to each moment as doing so creates additional limitations as they then become strengthened. Rather, might the desire be to shift and move into a more uplifting premise by shifting the focus? Put happier objectives into play when a shift is enlisted in this way.

If those aches and pains were gone, however, what have they to talk to others about and who are they without such issues? Is it that they acknowledge nothing more than the reflection they see in the mirror each morning? To routinely offer the same response to the often asked question, *How are you doing today?* is quite telling. Do you see in focusing on the same unwanted issues, in the same way, they reinforce and anchor those very things to their life?

Imagine if someone who had an illness or body condition answered the question, *How are you doing today?* by responding with something other than a detailed list of complaints about a failing body. Instead, if their response were: *I'm really doing well today* . . . (even though they were not). *I have truly enjoyed this wonderful morning. It was so refreshing to watch the sunrise. I saw all of the magnificent colors in the sky and was in awe of its beauty. I love to experience the sun as it rises each morning. What a beautiful morning!* Or, *I'm doing about the same, but I know I will have an inspired day today and look forward to the opportunities that await me.*

How does Universe engage with an optimistic person as opposed to someone who constantly reinforces illness and adversity in a rote and repetitive manner? How could their life ever change out of its current loop if they are unwilling to shift from their script a time or two? They have little possibility to alter their reality when they continually strive to reinforce it. This is unfortunate but true. Universe will return what is engaged in and focused upon within the mind.

All is in or out of Universal flow, and knowing this can help you experience life in a more effortless manner. Once you become anchored in the basics by establishing some fundamental knowledge, then you can begin to shift the way you look at things. You will be able to move more into the flow of how you wish your life to proceed. How you might easily move into a more desired space and the amount of effort, or effortlessness, needed to get you there. You are the creator of your storyline. It is through your desires and intentions that more will be given, offering options to get you closer to what is wanted. This will allow you to more readily connect to receive that which you seek as you move toward manifesting a new reality. What is meant by this?

In co-creating your world, might you look at your surroundings? Consider first how you present yourself. Although you may not have made your clothes, do you look at them as an extension of you? They are, in many ways, a projection of you in this physical dimension as they are often of your choosing. They evoke an understanding of who you are. The colors selected, the style, the variety are each a component of self-expression.

Let's look at your car. Although it may not be the vehicle you prefer, it, too, is a reflection of its owner. Do you keep it tidy, clean, and orderly, or is it cluttered and unkept? Is this also true of your home? Does everything have a specific location, or are some things scattered about here and there? So you see, all is mirroring back to the world who you are, for you are who? Although you might see an egoic premise, too, can you also see an overarching point to consider as well? And might we focus there now?

You will continually read here and must realize you are so much more than your physical form might cause you to believe. You will continue to see this sentiment stated here. Yet, will you muse and contemplate the following premise?

Your Spiritual Essence resides within and is tethered to your physical form for the duration of this life. It is here where so much is to be experienced and understood. You are more spiritual than physical. You came here, into human form, to experience life on this planet and what it is like to do and feel your creations.

If you came to experience certain human emotions, perhaps you chose to embody into a highly expressive family. In this way, you could experience the vast array of feelings at play within this sort of family dynamic and the emotionally charged environment it would elicit. You wanted to see how certain things felt from a perspective you devised before you entered into form. Isn't all experience an interpretation and understanding based upon collective experiences?

Might one say then that your perspectives are formulated based on those experiences you have had up and to this point? They provide you with a certain baseline proclivity to lean one way or the other as you formulate your decisions. When you see the world from your unique vantage, you are viewing life through your personalized set of rose-colored glasses.

Consider now an expanded understanding which continues beyond the sole premise such lens routinely imply.

Rose-Colored Glasses: These glasses represent how your world has been uniquely flavored by the understandings you have adopted in this lifetime. Flavored by what you have seen, heard, or felt. This is how the canvas of your life has been colored.

These glasses act as a filter and allow the individual to superimpose their unique set of beliefs into the mix of their daily dealings. So when something pops up and into play, the individual's vast history is utilized to give the wearer this or that perspective. It is this perspective that flavors how they perceive and receive what they see. This is the lens used to interpret any given situation.

And so, these glasses move the individual toward their intended purpose flavoring life in a way of positive reinforcement, yet perhaps unrealized in the same vein by another. This then impacts the experiences held and all that moves each to individually do and be.

So you see, these glasses are most important as they seek to move you in a more direct and purposeful way to reinforce and realize the vibrational component you seek to more fully know. This will enable you to perceive the options which feel better and to enable those things to become more readily accomplished.

Might we present this premise? Have you gone to a lecture and walked away with an interpretation of what was being conveyed? You may have heard the same lecture and lecturer as did others, but each attendee left with a different understanding of what was communicated. You may have picked up a significant amount of information yet only focused on those components that resonated with you, missing many other details given.

This is noteworthy in a couple of regards. Individuals isolate and focus upon those components that reinforce what they already believe. Yet miss equally important information. So while absorbing those things that reinforce existing beliefs, some other vitally important information is totally missed, dismissed, or misinterpreted. So it is interesting how the mind does pick and choose what it takes in. But in missing certain information conveyed, was it not yet time to hear that part of the message? All things are understood by you in the right time, the perfect time for you to receive that specific insight.

You are also in a time when spiritual discoveries are communicated and accepted more easily. It hasn't always been this way. So to be in this moment in time is quite a marvelous thing. Now, information is more readily available from a variety of sources and resources. All is so much more accessible.

It is also incredible to realize that not so long ago, technology dramatically shifted. Today, you can get directions, shop, and have an encyclopedia of knowledge accessed by your smartphone. Answer machines, paper maps, and encyclopedias are no longer as vital as before. So many things can be accomplished in a shorter amount of time. So imagine where this will lead and the discoveries that await further expansion. New inventions are being introduced each day. As you see, now is the time when so much more can be. Advancements seemingly occur overnight.

With the advent of smartphone electronics and other similar devices, it is so important to not only tune in to those things that will assist you to complete a task but to not lose sight of those components that elevate and raise your psyche. In turn, your physical being is assisted too. A functional body will enable you to reach additional levels of accomplishment. Seek to continually marvel at the wonders of your body. Your Spiritual Essence will thrive when you take control of your mind as it regulates your bodily functions. All will work in a more harmonious way when this occurs.

And remember to always seek to keenly discern what is before you. Discernment is a most necessary component for you to understand, engage, and employ. This is especially important as you navigate through various teachings to determine what is appropriate and truthful before you place your trust fully in them. Simple in premise and sometimes more difficult in practice, but this need not be. Know, too … you must shift and seek new avenues to explore when it is appropriate to move from one space to the next.

Sometimes solitude and inward reflection are beneficial but know it will be your work with others which will mark your time here. Know when it is time to operate from a more solitary posture and when it is time to engage. And, too, recognize you always have all you need. Such tools can be found upon your focus and intention to shift course.

Consider the following scenario. Imagine having arrived unexpectedly in a remote setting. Upon arriving, you must gather some basic tools to survive. You might locate items from resources available, but if you are on a deserted island, only certain things are of use in such a setting. So you have to deal with life at a more fundamental or basic level. You gather things to provide some measure of comfort, food, and protection from the elements. You meditate and seek to elevate your consciousness while there. Yet, in time, you want to return home and rejoin those you knew before becoming isolated. Perhaps you can share the inner strengths and insights gathered in the process. You have done all the meditation and internal work you can do, and although this is a most beautiful setting, you need to be back around others. So you recognize this temporary situation must end, although you sought to make the best of this experience. What steps might you take to reconnect you back to the general population?

You have built many fires for warmth and illumination, but now maybe a bonfire would be a better option. You recall reading about those who threw a bottle into the ocean with a message, but you don't have a cork. And where would you say you are anyway? How would this really help if you need to be found? Do you have a compass or any other sort of navigational device?

So what can be done to more quickly return you to where you seek to be? Well, it's taking other action based upon newly perceived options. You think through and realize no one is looking for you here, so merely surviving is not enough. You must shift your focus to realize a different reality. The one you see now doesn't have an outcome you like.

You devise a plan of action to bring you back to civilization. In it, you have to navigate through rough waters and get into the flow of the ocean's current. If you can get into its flow, you know you will have a much better chance of getting into a shipping channel, where people in vessels exist, and you can be found.

Once in the flow of the ocean's current, things seem to happen more fluidly, without the struggle or fight to go against its purposeful direction. Now you arrive in navigable waters. These waterways can get you to a desired destination faster while connecting you with others, more surely than before. And that is what we seek to impart here.

You can reach your destination more directly with less struggle when you enter the flow when in its current. But what happens when you've been engaged in life and didn't know of such things as Universal flow or even that it is beneficial to move from one thought to the next until you find one that feels a bit better? So here you are. You have experienced life and have been on a roller coaster ride that seemed wonderful one minute and a little scary the next.

Choices present themselves daily. When you do not know all the choices available, you choose from a more limited set of options. There are always at least two choices in every circumstance, right? But what if there were more than just two to select from at each crossroad? When you realize there are more options to consider with even better outcomes to be had, might those understandings be preferred? You will never know unless you strive to expand the world as you now see it. So as you make life decisions, create shortcuts today, rather than waiting until tomorrow to employ and enjoy them.

Yes, if you are reading this book, you are a seeker. As such you are looking for ingredients to enrich your life, to make it more meaningful, easier to navigate, and to enable preferred shifts to occur. Those shifts will occur as you strive to align into a space of wholeness and completeness.

Let us consider how you might lessen and ultimately remove pain and despair from your life. Is it possible to control aspects within your body and mind that before were solely relegated to your doctor's care? This is not to say you no longer need to consult and engage medical practitioners, but rather this is to alert you of the many unseen tools you've had available since birth. Seek to access those things which have been with you all along. They have been hidden from view but are accessible upon your focused attention. You see, your focus activates them.

You are a Spiritual Being who came to experience life on this planet. You were not dropped here by some unexplained means with the hope you might somehow survive the experience. Know that you came here with advanced knowledge but were you ever taught this concept … how to access these things or reconnect to them? You learned a lot of things in your youth, but were some of these points missing from your earlier upbringing?

How different would your life be if you knew through your focused attention, you could align with a vibrational frequency to change what exists today? Within this frequency, cells can be altered to out-picture a different body or circumstance. In this realm of existence, pain and physical shortcomings could be eliminated. Well, it is true. Reality is, and you are, as you believe them to be.

When negative stories are repeated, especially when recounted or shared in great detail, the situation is vibrationally recreated. So the life experience or body shortcoming is revived. In this scenario, each is given new life and actually becomes more anchored to re-engage with those thoughts as they are resuscitated. Surely, no one would knowingly do this.

So each time you talk about your aches and pains and more detail is given, think again. In this way, you tether their shortcomings to your world. Seek to limit complaints. Such diatribes only enlist to reinforce similar things to your current reality. So you see, it is very important to remain aware and to stay present and conscious throughout your day of what you think, do, and say. These are some fundamental steps for you to consider so you might operate routinely from a more conscious level, rather than retreating to past occurrences or, conversely, living in the future.

Yes, some future planning is important to do. A mention or reference to the past is understandable, but we advise not living a majority of your day mentally from a past or future perspective. Or not to attach to recurrent, unwanted thoughts daily. Stay grounded and aware of your present surroundings and activities. This is necessary to not become stuck and to more readily move forward. Do seek to maintain this level of understanding. Be and remain in the present moment by being present. This is key.

So what happens as you maintain presence in a world where so many are unaware of those things which surround their day? Would you see a miracle if it were to appear instantly before you? For that, you must be present. So often, slipping back to a future or past thought is a basis for one's reality. When this is so, notice it, then re-engage your awareness to the present moment and begin again. It is a retraining of sorts. We do support your efforts to become more conscious. And now, we seek to move forward beyond these basics and build upon them.

Living from another reality, other than one that resides in the flow, is exhausting. Do you seek to relive life with alternate realities? There are other teachings that you might consider, but for now, let us limit this discussion to past or future thinking where you engage in something other than the present moment. Again, we encourage you to be present in each moment and to remain consciously aware.

This can be difficult, but it need not be. Practice this … just begin by being present and staying aware of what is going on around you right now and when you move past these pages. If constant monitoring is needed, so you do not slip back into negative thinking, let us implement a zippy mind game.

Mind Game

Sit for a moment in a comfortable way and clear your mind. Now recall past patterns, the memories that keep coming back to you, and when they arrive this time, speed them up. See them zip through your mind's eye almost like they are on a conveyor belt, and now flip the switch and see the frames of thought speed up even more. See the experiences move so quickly through the filter of your mind that it is hard to make out what is occurring or being said. It will take you out of those repetitious thoughts and move you into another space. You can make it comical, too, if you like, depending on your mood and preference. You can have fun with this practice. The best part is you will shift out and into a new mental space.

Now that you've taken a bit of a break to practice, do you feel a bit lighter and free from the treadmill of thought?

If you've not stopped to practice, please do so now

In making light of a burden, you shift its hold on the mind. To engage and even play with this mentally, you engage in a mind game of sorts when you outwit the wit. Do you see you can make folly of the weightiness such thoughts make and might impose upon you? And in doing so, their impact is lessened. Surely, as you make light of such advancements of the mind, you disarm it. You play the game as you choose and not of its choosing. So you weaken the mind's grasp and grip and lighten the load it would levy. It is a burden to carry such heavy thoughts around with you, moment by moment, day by day. So when the mind decides to take you on a journey beyond the present moment, seeks to take you down a murky path, just stop. Be observant. Be aware. Be present. Then, play a mind game with your mind.

What about when a future occurrence is placed in your path, and you see something that is fearful to consider? It certainly is a possibility for this fearful thing to become a reality in your life, but other realities are also possible. Maybe you are in between jobs, and you wonder if you will have enough money to pay your rent or perhaps to put food on your table. You do have money in the bank, but what if something happens and now that money isn't enough to sustain you? What if? What if you find another job and it's something you've always wanted to do, and what if you now have more than enough money to buy everything you could want and more? And so it goes.

There are so many options for what might occur in your future. Perhaps focus on establishing some good intentions. Then feel the happiness that occurs when you lay claim to the better thoughts they produce. Isn't it better to think good thoughts and have those turn into your new reality than to place too much weight on what you want to avoid? As you focus and feel, you create what can be. Remember, you are the creator of your reality. So why not choose a better one than yesterday?

How might this book provide insights, guidance, and knowledge so you might manifest a new course of action? If you find new ideas here, how will you put action behind these words? Don't just check off another book from your to-do list. Simply reading these words and placing this book back onto your bookshelf, to try out another day is not recommended. How will this book assist you if you don't enlist some of its measures to change things up a bit?

Enlist the steps interspersed here. These are the initial ones you might implement today. Your recognition to take any step, well, that's the first step. Perhaps test them out as you go. In taking action now, you build upon what is communicated here … by your works. How do you know which steps will work for you unless you implement them? Only by implementing and doing can you recognize those steps that become key to assist you in what you want to shift. Maybe, put just one concept into play and see where it leads you. This might be one of many initial changes you want to make. Rather than simply reading these words, act upon them.

FIND THE PORTAL OF CHANGE THAT AWAITS ACTIVATION WHEN YOU SEEK TO EVOKE A DIFFERENT OUTCOME

We intend to introduce those concepts that will cause you to pause, and so we also hope you do not race through these pages but rather see how one task resonates for you and transitions you into a better space of being. Never before have we so stressed, for we see a much-driven society and many who speed through the day without being present in it.

Track Your Progress

Your time here on Earth is most precious. Implement the small steps outlined within these pages to maximize the potential of what might be shifted to create new possibilities and outcomes within your life. Decide today to be present in each moment so you can begin to recognize and personify who you will become as you re-engage with life from a different vantage.

Chapter 4

Expansive Love

There are verses and mantras which can help you focus and slow the mind from its wandering and unending banter. Breathing is a simple method used to slow the mind when you place your focus there. And deep breaths allow for an expanded awareness to be realized. Will you take some deep breaths now? Breathe in and out. Taking deep breaths to the count of 1-2-3 as you breathe in, then count 1-2-3 as you breathe out. In and out. In and out . . . measured and deep. Place your hand on your diaphragm to make sure you are breathing deeply and not merely taking shallow breaths.

Deep breathing is most important when you enter into meditation or when taking in new understandings. In taking deep breaths, you allow for a better integration to occur, which will facilitate greater clarity to be realized, as an inner knowingness is felt.

And so, we now move into a significant discussion, the deeper meaning of Love. Its true meaning is of greater scope and value than you may currently be aware.

How might love be expanded upon? We say that love opens hearts so that with this added measure, Love can be integrated as it is internalized and can exponentially flourish within as it moves beyond your physical form into the world. As you express Love with the intention to employ a renewed understanding, you release an added spark of Love into the physical world. This Love will move mountains, so to speak, as it is expressed fully internalizing and utilizing its expansive meaning and vibration.

Once this vibrational component is put into play, Love can be brought into your world for use once again as it was intended. Its vibration will blossom and grow within you. We know when you cognitively embrace, employ, and feel its all-encompassing frequency in its limitless form, you will begin to engage with the full measure of what it seeks to impart. Let the vibratory component we discuss become a part of how you feel toward each thing in this world of form.

This deeper realization will not only expand the feelings associated with this routinely described emotion, it will also allow you to utilize it energetically, in that it is so much more. Each level of understanding will grow its scope as you apply it within your daily dialog. When you utilize Love in its fuller capacity, it will be engaged from a higher vibrational frequency. Cognitively, as you associate the word you knew before as a more specifically defined love, move now to engage Universal Love. As you begin to utilize and apply its expansive meaning, you will employ its higher vibrational energy.

So your communications with others will engage them and you with a higher frequency, utilizing this higher vibration when you knowingly express and invoke this Love. As you think of its unbounded means and speak now of Love, a new vibrational resonance emerges. This energy will shift many things, including you.

The first immediate change will be the creation of a more expansive you, as this empowered Love will resonate within your body upon your intentioned focus. It will generate a more elevated frequency or feeling, changing how you vibrationally resonate. All who come into contact with it will shift accordingly. There is a faster vibration that emanates at this level of understanding. When connecting to this expansive frequency, you will begin to feel the difference as you internalize and engage with it; as you look at this often used word a bit differently. From this point forward, set an intention to utilize its more illuminating and potent form as you allow its fuller measure to be experienced. Might you recognize the expansive scope we now discuss?

So do you see with this one expanded interpretation or understanding, Love grows (love → Love) exponentially as you express it. The expansion occurs within the frequency potential. Everything moving outward from its vibration is exponentially impacted, touched, or imprinted upon in a new way.

Clear your mind as we share what was given in **The Little Book to Find Your Purpose** –

So do recognize you have a Loving Aspect that wants your every success. Universe, God, Father, Mother all are terms for the Higher Source that seeks to offer direction and guidance. We recognize the term love is underutilized and not always connected to the unlimited potential of Universal Love. Engage now with its fuller measure to energetically evoke a vibrational frequency, unlike any other. Engage with this frequency in a more conscious way.

Love is indeed an emotion. But it is so much more than what most routinely associate with it. When its full efficacy is discovered upon the broader interpretation, it is consciously internalized and put into play. With this understanding, Love can become more expansive when you release its vast energy as you engage with it in this way. Call it into action within your world and into this physical octave with intention and purpose as you squarely place your focus upon utilizing it in its fuller measure and limitless potential.

What do we mean by this? Love has an energetic vibration that elevates and raises the vibratory frequency when it is consciously called into being. This activates its unique and expansive healing potential. When tapping into love this way, at this level, when you invoke this Love, it evokes an accelerated frequency.

So when you align with Love and the aspect of Love as you focus upon it now, rather than engaging its more common definition, you can enter into Love's all-encompassing vibration as your energy is buoyed into another vibrational frequency. If you have not felt this in the past, you might pause to feel this energy as you consciously invoke it now.

Your energy reacts to match its vibration, as will anything which comes into contact with it. As it moves out into the world of form, it will elevate the vibration of everything in its path before returning back to you.

Seek to no longer limit Love or simply equate it to a physical emotion — an emotion that defines a certain way to feel toward another person or thing. Recognize and now feel how Father and Mother Earth feel toward all of Earth's inhabitants, how the Angelic Kingdom feel toward humankind, how Beings of Light, Universe, God feel toward all creatures from all Kingdoms. By taking this one intentional step, a frequency is created that resonates differently. Tap into this frequency by consciously feeling their Love and focused devotion. Do so by coordinating your mind's eye with your heart center. Through this combined action, in time, you will feel the full efficacy and expansiveness of this Love.

It is from this perspective that you might now express this word and draw all of its kind back to you as it then moves out into the world. It is through the full circle approach of bringing back, complete unto you, what you have put forth as it increases accordingly. When you feel the effect of what you have introduced vibrationally, you will understand its limitless expanse.

This vibrational aspect has been readily accessible yet not often consciously employed in recent times. Now with this one added understanding, more is offered, and its true potential can be realized. Consciously utilize, engage, and invoke this concept of Love. See the results of this energy when purposefully introduced once again into the physical realm.

Expansive opportunities await as you recognize the ability to engage all of life and Universe from a different vantage. From this stance, you can move mountains within your world and thus reap any desired outcome more quickly than before.

All of life wants your success; wants you to have all you seek. Wants you to find what has remained hidden for a time, and with your continued focus, conscious Love, and devotion … can you now see how all is truly possible?

Even the spin of an atom can be recalibrated when engaged to utilize a different vibrational frequency.

All is energy, vibration, frequency.

And so it is.

Align with the following Verse and its verses, which will immerse you in Love's healing components —

I call now for every cell, atom, electron within my being to be refreshed and made whole once again. I see every component as whole and healed. I recognize and Love each microscopic element within this body and do send my body Love and healing this moment, this day.

I am so grateful for all my body does in its support of my Spiritual Being and world. I send a tidal wave of Love to it and through it now, filled with gratitude and immersed in the vibration of Universal Love.

I am so grateful for all components of my life, and all this body has produced through its unending service to my Spiritual Being. I give gratitude for all it does provide me. I now seek divine insights to provide my body with the necessary resources to enable its pain-free functionality. I enlist its continued support as I work to heal all that is in need of repair.

How can healing best occur, and how can I do or enact those steps which will allow this body to self-heal and continue to manifest health and wholeness moving forward in Light and Love? I surrender to Universe all that is needed to fulfill this request.

Let it be so — and So It Is.

Utilizing Love's expansive potentiality, send Love to all body parts now. See it as an energetic wave blanketing your body in deep, rich color. Bathe your body in Love as you see each limb, cell, and component fully immersed in its expansive vibrational energy. Feel its sufficiency, healing properties, and presence. Then believe as you fully feel and affirm this Verse, again, to immerse your body in the healing vibration of Universal Love.

This day, it is especially incumbent to remember you are much more than this physical form. This body serves to host your Essence, and it is a physical tool to facilitate and enable you to accomplish what you are destined to do and be in this life. So look at your body as you would clothing to put on and wear each day. This is the purpose of your physical form. Know it will serve you well. And like mending a garment in need of repair, it, too, can be repaired and restored so you might continue with its full functionality and use.

Know too, sometimes, it is time to put on a new garment, especially when delayed repairs have allowed advanced deterioration to occur. To start with a garment that is fresh and new is sometimes a better course of action to allow for a new set of experiences to be enjoyed. But for now, let us focus on making improvements and modifications to this body, which serves as your temple as it hosts your Spiritual Essence. Seek to restore your body to a level which will allow for its continued use as you move closer toward achieving each desired objective.

Chapter 5

Now That You Know

You are embodied here for only a brief time. What understandings can we share to make your experience more effective and valuable, so a purposeful change and exchange might occur? Consider the benefits of healing conditions such as eating disorders that might otherwise create shortcomings in your physical form.

As you know, diet is very important, and you must realize so much can be and is affected by what you eat. There are authors who can provide you with insights to make more enlightened food choices and those who can offer healthy recipes. Do become more educated on dietary points, especially when food is used as a crutch. Delve into understanding the issues at play within your own psyche when food is used in this way.

Does eating provide a means of comfort to some? Ingesting large quantities of food appears to be an insulation mechanism to create more layers of protection from the outside world. Layering encompasses various levels of understanding. In many cases, a layering of issues is compounded by a layering of cells, as both components work to protect and guard against something entering in.

Know the ingredients of the food you eat and how they are prepared. Unfortunately, cutting corners to make more of a monetary return often occurs in food preparation. In this fast-paced society, homemade foods are probably more of a rarity. We hope, however, you will find ways to seek out those restaurants, or food groups, where healthier choices exist. You may have to pay more for quality meals, but take steps to protect, as well as nourish, this long-term investment. Invest in yourself in this way.

Be a wise custodian of what you put into your body. Your car is fueled with the appropriate octane to maximize its operation and continued performance. Know, too, you must treat your body with at least as much respect as your automobile, so it will continue to take you where you want to go. We know you seek to maximize your activities in this life, so take good care of your body to ensure and boost its performance. Seek to maximize how the body functions by feeding it the proper fuel. If this concept were taken to heart, more individuals would seek to implement some different dietary choices to enable quick and verifiable results.

So what can we offer that you might implement to make a difference rather quickly? Imagine a flame. There is a fire which exists within your form, and when invoked, it can grow in significance, relevance, and scope. You've heard the phrase, *when life is snuffed out,* or some other reference to a fire within. But we tell you there is significance to acknowledging it. It is your connection to your Higher Being, and this connection can be made more significant each day. As you elevate and expand the Flame within your form, you will see measured improvements in your body's ability to function, allowing for a more effortless flow to occur within.

Take a moment. Clear your mind. Become and stay centered as you read Flame Ignite.

Flame Ignite

L ife for me is very precious.
It is a reflection of my inner me.
As I see life and all its wonders,
let me bask in that which sets me free.
Free from pain and consequence;
free from energetic woes.
Free from doubt and consternation;
free from all that I do now let go.

I AM open to forgiveness, not from others, but from self.
I do now see how this holds the key to unlock my full,
expansive potentiality.

Bring that Aspect that lies hidden,
dormant less expansive now,
to engage and resurrect It
as It moves throughout me now.
There is but a small Flame burning;
It is yet a mere glow.
Let me elevate Its yearning, as I invoke It,
It does now grow.

Consume all that feels downtrodden,
less than the full potential I AM to Be.
I know my life will be more centered
to flow in grace synergistically.

Flame Ignite
(continued)

I release doubt, remorse, fear as I let my story out.
It is there, amongst the Flame
    which now begins to dance about.
Let me stoke this glowing Ember
    as It strengthens with delight.
It is a light so bright and bold,
    I AM so grateful to behold the Love It does ignite.

Always present, yet now so bright.
It has waited to fully ignite
    Its beautiful flame of colors bright
    that now do quiver and quake with delight.
See the flutter, do you see It growing exponentially?
It is no longer my hidden treasure,
    for now to It I do lay claim.
I realize that God Source resides within
    as I watch the momentum, it begins.

Yes, this Flame resides within me for sure
    as It expands this day and burns ever pure.
For as I acknowledge my connection to Source,
    Universal Love floods in and through to thus reinforce
    as Love and Light do merge to Ignite,
    transmute and go forth.

Flame Ignite
(continued)

To enable this flow, I know this to be true to my core
 and believe as never before.
In this knowing, I will resolve to restore
 all that's amiss and so much more.

I acknowledge, Love and do nurture this Flame.
In this connection to God Source I do now remain.
It does emblazon me within,
 as I feel Its Light and Its Love
 which empowers my being
 to strengthen my life force from below to above.

In knowing and being,
 I do reinforce and recognize that in due course,
 all will lessen,
 dissolve and no longer burden my life force.

Flaming, pulsating, the Fire that did shimmer
 now burns and expands to run like a river.
The flow does move to heal and restore
 as It strengthens my foundation down to my core.

I feel this, know and believe Love is key.
As all Aligns within to now set me free.

In these words, you will find keys that can be integrated to advance improvements within. As time permits, read Flame Ignite again and often before moving into your activities. In taking these small steps and, more importantly, internalizing these words, you will emblazon the Flame within. Much will be enabled to flow in and to you when you resonate with this concept and believe. And know, too, healing is the ultimate objective of these pages as we look to create the means to allow for shifts to occur.

Now awaken what has resided within you (all along) to open, expand, and flourish. You see, you would not be here on this planet, stranded, so to speak, without all the necessary tools to successfully navigate this terrain. You can access each and every tool that will more readily enable you to accomplish your dreams and desires. To fully manifest those desired things, connect and open up to each possibility when you believe. Your belief will make it so.

DO YOU BELIEVE THIS

CAN YOU FEEL AND KNOW THIS
TO BE UNQUESTIONABLY TRUE

ALL LIES WITHIN AND CAN BE ACCESSED
WHEN THIS UNDERSTANDING IS FULLY EMBRACED,
ACKNOWLEDGED, AND KNOWN BY YOU TO BE SO

THIS IS KEY

Over time, many tools and their corresponding understandings were hidden, misinterpreted, and ultimately, access to them was lost … for they could not be seen. Now seek for such recall as you re-engage them into this day. This is an enlightened time where buried treasures resurface and so seek to unearth part of your heritage. In this vein, Universe also engages through your thoughts, words, and corresponding actions of support. These actions of support are those that reinforce your convictions and beliefs. Engage and connect to those things you wish to bring forward into the Nowness of this time. Seek to move into an aligned oneness to express and out-picture all that awaits manifestation.

Once you have reconnected to those things which are yours to claim, you will have access to a wealth of abilities that will enable you to do and be as never before. So you see, with just a few more tools to add to your toolkit, you will have practices that will expand this life and heal aspects in need of a slight tweak to maximize and allow for your body's greater performance.

Might we practice and play a bit right now? What habit or practice do you employ frequently? Some eat snacks, some pick their fingers, while some have other such attributes to which they lay claim. We seek to remove or to shift one such thing in your life today, and in so doing, we believe your life will change immeasurably.

So now, what might you change? What action do you perform in a somewhat mindless manner? Is it to snack on chips, to inflict pain by picking, or chewing on your fingers, or to simply twirl your hair? What would it be? What would you like to focus on now and change? You have the power to enact change with just a couple of additional points of consideration.

Let's make a decision now and know you can add other ones to the mix later. What about watching television? Do you engage there and become unresponsively lost in its banter? Do you drink? Do you seek now to release engagement with some unnecessary thing? And so, what might you seek to release this day? Might you focus here for a time as you pause your mind in a meditative way?

Imagine peeling an onion. Place what you wish to resolve in the middle of the onion. Do you see any activity coming out of the peel? Can you barely see it, somewhat grayed out, but its essence emerging? Look closely. See those periods of doing this, that or the other, when you are not being fully present in the moment. You have checked out for a bit and are going into a habit. Where have you gone? Isn't a habit something done almost ritualistically without thinking? Seek to remain present.

In the future, should you move to do this thing, engage awareness into the mix of this activity. In staying present, shift and move into a space of presence. Does the habit you seek to release fit within the framework we have described? If you agree with the parameters in place, let us proceed. If not, let's play with another. Focus on just this one habit for a time. See the onion peel and know this is the framework established to open up and reveal what has been done without seeing, thinking, or even fully feeling.

Maybe you've checked out for a bit. Recognize this, and seek to no longer move in an unconscious manner. Now consciously look at this issue with fresh eyes. With this new sight, see what could not be completely recognized or acknowledged before. Let those things which pop out of the onion be significant ones to provide you with keys to know what was intrinsically given and felt by you in this experience … as you now choose to know more directly without the burden of the habit. How does this activity make you feel? Will you focus here for a few minutes? Then we will add more for your consideration.

WHAT HAPPENED BEFORE YOU DRIFTED
INTO THIS HABIT

WHAT LED YOU TO IT

DETERMINE WHAT ACTION OR ACTIONS HAVE
CAUSED YOU TO WANT TO ESCAPE
FROM YOUR CURRENT SURROUNDINGS

Consider what you choose to focus upon initially, as a more basic issue might be a bit easier to resolve. Use something simple to give you a bit of practice before tackling a more difficult undertaking. Yet, if this one issue has been engaged for a long time and you seek for its release, let us start there.

If it is a long-standing issue, stay focused and engaged to allow each ingredient to be sufficiently uncovered as you peel away and expose its core premise. If this is the most significant of your issues, continue this work over time, especially if you find it more challenging and multilayered. If there are many layers to uncover, this may take a bit of practice to allow for all of its components to surface.

Maybe different things occur in your surroundings which have caused you to engage in this habit. You may have to consider each from different vantages at various points in time. The key is to become aware of the feelings that moved you to practice this mindless thing and why this state of being is preferred. As you place your focus and keen attention on this, the feelings that led to this action will become known because it is the connection with the feeling that was sought. The familiarity of the feeling was achieved when you went into this rote activity.

Perhaps let us consider fingerpicking. Some pick their fingers or cuticles routinely, but picking to provide comfort is a dichotomy of sorts, as this sort of practice is painful. But when you fall into a rote state of doing something unconsciously, which we suggest here, you move out of the conscious engagement of it and into a mindless practice. As you engage here, you move into a space of not thinking, and perhaps, not fully feeling. Is it plausible then to believe this pain might register differently? Do comfort and familiarity enter into the equation as these things are felt in the process? Comfort in the control perceived, and familiarity in the frequency of its occurrence.

In this exercise, we seek for you to re-engage with the present moment, which brings in awareness and allows for different choices to be made. This will occur as you give up complacency or mindless pursuits. We seek to provide information so that alternate activities can be enacted as opposed to indulging in this sort of comfort. To reintroduce a means which will allow you to move beyond what is currently a part of your life, yet not preferred.

Can you consciously change one aspect in your life by your intent to do so? Let us add a bit more to this premise. Can you allow a degree of peace, from the chatter of the mind, to enter into the mix? A mantra and verses were provided within the understandings imparted in our *Little Book* so you might slow and still the mind. Would it also be of value to discuss such insights here?

When slowing the mind, you have the ability to move more seamlessly to accomplish each task. In this way, you lessen the mind's grip and its incessant directives while not imposing ego's sharp criticisms. Without the unrelenting ramblings that occur mentally, your decisions may take you on a different path — one that is more inspired and uplifted.

As you sit in a comfortable position, what peaceful measures can we introduce or reintroduce? Engage once again in a meditative way. Clear your mind to allow peace to engulf you like a blanket. In blanketing you with its serenity, feel the thickness and weighty quality of this oh-so-soft blanket as it envelopes you in Love. See it covering your body and giving you comfort and peace. Feel it fully and see it in a muted, soothing color. The frequency is slower but not lower.

Now move forward to embrace additional measures to clear your life of unwanted nuances and to effect change within your entire being. For this to be accomplished, we ask also if you are interested in finding a calmness you might retain? A calmness where you seek for the mind to be slowed and not so anxious in its pursuit of the next accomplishment. Visualize to incorporate this measure into your practice.

Remain in meditation for a time, as you feel the full measure of Love blanketing, as it envelopes you.

Universe seeks your happiness if that is what you wish to find. Does happiness lie in the advent of finding cures or the means to remedy a situation? You might find in slowing the mind, much can be accomplished. It is one of the best ways to allow for healing to occur. When the mental push/pull is slowed to allow for other things to enter into your awareness, a pause is offered. This allows you to engage life from a different and more positive vantage.

LOOK UPON THE MIND AS A TOOL

When ego engages with the mind to maintain its foothold within your world, you must determine if it has a valid reason to do so. Much of ego's original premise is no longer necessary, and so you must guard and restrict its play upon you. Seek to minimize what plays and repeats in the background of your mind. Perhaps re-engage now to monitor the mind and then eliminate unnecessary banter by remaining present in this moment and each one that follows.

We will soon provide details and discuss the benefits of an exercise intended to disengage a looping mechanism. Use this method when you recognize the mind to be occupied in this way. It can be implemented when you want to remove something continually looping and playing mentally. In removing certain undesired scenes, you can deactivate to stop its ability to loop when you seek to still or slow it. However, monitoring your thoughts and having continued awareness of what runs within means remaining conscious and being present to what pops into play.

Do you understand why remaining consciously aware and engaged in the present moment to be key as we progress? To move in any other manner would mean you are not doing so from a centered and whole perspective. This is so in that you lose the value and connection found there. It is in the present moment where you can enlist and seek change to enter in. This is where the healing process can be more readily engaged.

Chapter 6

Invoking Change

How might you begin to self-heal? And specifically, how can you heal your body and your immediate world? What might be done? We do not propose here for you to limit seeing doctors. Rather, we would encourage you to continue eliciting multiple medical opinions as you search for answers to why your body is doing thus and such. Why you feel as you do, and what can be done to enact positive change.

Do you truly seek to change certain health components that exist currently in your life? Whether you want new mental constructs or a better functioning body, do you want to shakeup how things are going? So what do you need to do in order to invite change into the mix; to invite in those things which will lead to wholeness within your immediate world?

Consider now that Universal law determines how things will come to you based upon your thoughts and desires. Emotions and pain dictate those things which have come to help you define and determine your preferences of what you do or do not want. So how do you maintain good thoughts or feelings, and how do you stop your focus from returning to those negative ones? You do so by monitoring your thoughts and shifting to those that feel better.

So how does mental monitoring alter your current reality? And do the resulting changes actually promote healing in a way that can be readily seen? Yes, these are important considerations and the main purpose of this book. We seek to enlist healing to begin within your body and life. Will you seek to heal and bring wholeness to those things that are currently out of step with your expectations? Do you want to see some changes come about today? If this is your intent, then you can create a revised landscape.

So has pain served its purpose to show you those life choices which are not preferred? If your current situation no longer matches up with what you long for, seek a new outcome. Seek to experience a different reality. Do you no longer wish to remain within the status quo you had experienced before? Perhaps now you seek redirection. Pain and suffering have had their purpose as they adjusted your focus. They allowed a pause to occur and for you to engage from a new vantage. Perhaps now you see things from a perspective where you can more readily embrace some needed change. But issues have developed in conjunction with the pain and suffering, and they need to be shifted too. So what can be done to reframe your world so all of the components at play are those you want? How might a shift alter your focus and allow for new possibilities and their opportunities to unfold?

You see, all of life seeks your direction. Even misaligned cells, which formed in response to formerly held thoughts, seek new directives. How do you move away from those old precepts to allow for something else to become the more dominant directive? You have played in the field of creation, and now you want another, more healthy manifestation to come forth. Everything is energy and that which flows from there. As such, when you change the frequency that resonates within your field, a shift can occur. This shift has the ability to grow in prominence and strength as you seek change to enter in.

FIGHT NOTHING

It has been said, and many exclaim: *fight this or fight that* as their preferred mantra. Let's look at the word *fight*. You can look up the definition, but for simplicity, it is used to describe what you do not want, what you do in war, what you want to get rid of, and aligns itself with push/pull energy or struggle. Pushing against what is. So one might say, *Fight war. Fight drugs. Fight cancer.* Although these are all catchy, short descriptive phrases, are they what you want to draw back more of, at any time, or could other less forceful words be engaged instead?

Perhaps refer to fighting against the onslaught of an illness in a different way. Especially because the energetic resonance of the word fight emits a frequency that draws back to itself like-kind vibrations. It goes out into Universe and returns back to the originating source with more energy of its kind. Use the words you want more of within your life — the words that, when multiplied by Universe, will return a similar but beneficial, vibratory frequency.

Why fight anything? You will find that working from a space of Love to be more beneficial. What Love will enable has no end. Choose Love instead of going against the flow of life, for fighting anything is not the best course of action.

Since beginning this book, your understandings have grown. As you proceed from this space, you can embrace and energetically move from a different place. Isn't it easier to ride the waves of life and find value in each activity as it moves you forward, rather than trying to stay in the same place as you brace yourself for the waves that break upon you? When you try to stand your ground, rather than to make necessary adjustments, do you risk injury and misstep as you stand in the ever-shifting sands of time?

Gratitude

At this juncture, we move to discuss the importance of gratitude as it is especially important to these works. Gratitude allows you to be in a different mental space. Gratitude is such a big component to your present moment that we take time here to focus on this one word. So let us pause to discuss its significance as it engages your emotions to shift how you align with the day. As such, does your day begin in gratitude? If it did not start that way today, will you yet pause to give gratitude this day?

Gratitude has a vast and momentous vibration. When you acknowledge and are thankful to Universe for what you are being shown, how you are being directed, what you are experiencing, more of that energy will be gathered and returned to you. It does have an unlimited multiplier effect. So as you surrender to this limitless multiplier, it acts as a gateway to expand the benefits experienced within the day. Recognizing this expansive portal will bring untold benefits into your life. Expressing and feeling gratitude daily will change the flow of your day and allow for different dynamics to be put into play. You might find ending and beginning each day with this vibrational multiplier most beneficial. It will shift all, especially you, when touched by its expansive reach.

Finding gratitude within your life is key. In time, you will find there is value in each seemingly unwanted nuance that occurs there. The fun is when you also discover and recognize the blessings these occurrences provide. Awaken to this understanding as you acknowledge them through gratitude. Yes, it is true that even disease and illness give you new insights and can show you the need for a course correction. So fight nothing and bless all things as you learn new insights and pathways toward deeper meanings and their understandings.

Have you already found that gratitude seems to offer a Universal portal to you? In this opening, look for the next ocean wave that will carry you in its current to what is next desired.

BEGIN YOUR DAY WITH GRATITUDE

DO TARRY IN BED BEFORE RISING TO EXPRESS GRATITUDE FOR YESTERDAY AND TODAY

Fifteen minutes before you get up in the morning is the perfect time for you to create a most necessary platform to align with the coming day. When you give gratitude, you begin creating a framework for the day. Let Universe know what is important to you. Start and end each day by envisioning those things you prefer to be a part of your life. This will let Universe know what you want more of, as more of that is returned to you.

When you journal or state in thought your points of gratitude, there is no second-guessing. This spells things out in a most specific way. If you went to bed dissatisfied or unhappy and awoke in that same manner the next morning, it would seem you want more of that sort of emotional drama in your life. So more of it is given. Once you elicit in gratitude what you truly want more of in a clearly defined way, you allow for more preferred things to be drawn to you.

With this understanding, do you find satisfaction as you begin to move into a space that will propel you toward your preferred path? Your focused desire will move to connect you to your purpose more readily as you tap into this energy. We see you are moving closer to that expression now. And for that, we express our gratitude of what might be for you as all does progress beyond this point in time.

So, with gratitude, you elicit a different flow of energy that will impact your day's activities. In this way, you invite Universe to be a part of your day. Your vibration shifts to align differently than before seeking to identify with it.

Try this fun exercise and perhaps utilize it routinely in your future. Focus on today's meetings and any upcoming scheduled appointments. Is there a particular outcome you would like to see occur? If so, might we suggest for you to envision each activity, the scheduled meetings, and each preferred outcome? See smiling faces, a handshake, a nod of agreement, or however you might best *Frame the Day* (AdvancedEnergetics.org). See each vividly. Now live the day as if you had already experienced that meeting or activity; proceed as if each had already taken place. Can you do this? Can you shift your energy to embrace something that hasn't actually happened yet, while mentally seeing each occurrence result as you intend? Can you feel the elation as if you were recalling this preferred outcome? Add a qualifier phrase to the visualized request. Then give gratitude for its successful conclusion.

In this way, there is no second-guessing. Universe will work to provide you with your request. You see, in this little exercise, you have also (individually) shifted energetically, and others will adjust their energy accordingly. They will engage with you at your new energetic level as you emanate a bit differently now. It will throw them off a little, especially if you've not operated from this vibrational level before. Yet, they will adjust to this new energetic blueprint. You see, you have created a newly preferred pathway. Thus, the changes, exchanges, and energy flow will shift to allow for all you seek to come into play.

Behind the Scenes

Have you ever considered other issues that occur behind-the-scenes? Do you find opposition awaiting your achievements; opposition to reaching and sustaining your desired aspirations? Have you accomplished and reached one of your many goals only to have it fail? Do you wonder why it seems you worked so hard to get the position or job promotion only to watch it unravel around you? You knew it wouldn't last, didn't you? Why is that? It was what you had aspired to accomplish for many years, and now it lies in ruins at your feet. *How can this be? Why did this happen?*

It's hard to handle when a cherished and notable achievement doesn't end as you might have preferred. It might rattle your confidence when something beautiful and fragile is dashed aside … crushed from the weight of its fall. But you are not made of crystal, and the pieces of your life aren't impossible to recast. Might you see the direction given to alter your steps in another way?

You have been gifted with knowledge, for these signs are surely gifts. So don't let the gift control you in a negative way. See the beauty in each thing you encounter and then move back into your day to reframe what appeared to be taken from you. Now realize its true meaning as you move into the space of gratitude … for this situation came to show you a new direction or path. Can you see this and step into a space of gratitude in the recognition of it now?

You see, you have conscious and subconscious workings which occur within simultaneously. Do you want this thing because it's the next natural step to take in your career path? Is this the best or only job option available to you? Is it what you want? Yes, it provides you with good financial stability, and isn't that a most necessary component? Well, then, you move into this mode and take on this role. But what if your subconscious has different plans and is (still) focused upon your more deeply held desires? A different sort of criteria was in play behind-the-scenes because you almost seemed to be working against yourself in this new role. So all the while you were striving in one direction, the subconscious was moving you away from it. Both directions were sought simultaneously, and both were moving seamlessly against … the other.

This dynamic is the self-saboteur. It's very frustrating to experience things such as this when the gift given isn't recognized. There are hidden components at play which create a push/pull momentum of internal opposition. Can you see this more clearly as you consider this now?

THE SUBCONSCIOUS WORKS IN TANDEM WITH UNIVERSE

All of the mind's determination will not change what you had set into motion before you took embodiment here. When mental victories occur, and they are not in keeping with your true path, you will not feel comfort or satisfaction when success arrives at your door. No comfort or solace is felt when you move away from what you were meant to do or be — what you earlier sought to experience from this life.

Many individuals, including you, may not yet know their purpose. They may feel unhappy or unsatisfied when they have not connected to that inner knowing or don't know how to discover their next step. We wish we could say each person will readily know what was outlined, yet the degree of angst experienced, especially when insights are missed, is most evident. Do you see signs along the way? Do you resist acknowledging or moving in sequence with them because they do not line up with what you've mentally mapped out for your future?

If you do not see them, might you slow down now and recognize insights given? They are surely there, and you are not seeing them in your haste. It is important to note when you seek to be given insights, guidance, or direction that they are not merely words you recite. Do you ask for help without intending for an answer to be provided? Once your words are uttered or strongly felt in your ponderings, do you search, seek out, or intently wait for a response? Do you have a vested interest and the expectation for answers to arrive?

You must be willing to sleuth out answers provided as they are surely there in response to your queries. But have you moved on? When you asked and not seeing or recognizing an instantaneous answer, did you move onto something else? But we tell you the call does elicit an answer. Were you too busy or preoccupied to slow down, pause, or listen to what was given? It was there for we know this to be so without question.

We could share stories where for days, if not months, some wander around with so much frustration as they never get out of their minds long enough to see new options that await their recognition. They are blocking other opportunities through their frustration while they continue to look through a more limited lens.

So let us ask, have you ever wandered about looking for something you later discovered to be holding in your hand? Or perhaps you nearly tripped on this thing after your search proved futile. Maybe you missed seeing (or even feeling) another seemingly lost thing as it was perched on top of your head. You searched and searched and couldn't find what was about you all along. And the frustration was further magnified when you discovered how each was so easily located and always within reach.

DO YOU READILY SEE WHAT IS BEFORE YOU

We tell you these things were messages given from a Higher Source. And it is quite simply you are not seeing what is before you. When this happens again, stop and think about what you have recently asked and how this occurrence might play into those dynamics. What important situation is now in your life that you are not fully seeing, not seeing all you might see, need to see? Many believe this sort of thing is relegated to forgetfulness, and some believe it to be relegated to age or age-related. We tell you to think again.

The mind is good at turning things around and getting you off-track. So play a mind game with your mind. Interpret these occurrences differently. See each as a response to a question or an insight given when having sought guidance. Consider, too, if you have rushed through the day and missed signs in your midst. Each are meant to help you navigate through a circumstance needing your attention. When trapped in the mind, you don't see the answers given or other recognizable indicators in your midst.

And so, why is the response not lining up with your expectations? Do you believe you have the best insights for your life and future? Is it impossible to think there may be an even greater opportunity for you to experience? Are you limiting what Universe might provide? Do you believe it's possible that something greater might await you? Might you qualify each request with something that will give Universe, and you, a little wiggle room to play in the field of possibility. Might you add wording such as ". . . or might Universe provide something better still" after each request?

By relinquishing control, you offer Universe another option. Do you see, you may think you know all the choices and what the next best step would be, but this may not be so. What if you are not recognizing all of your options? So if Universe is allowed to interject something more, then you are allowing more to be. Sometimes, the job you want is not the right fit, the love interest is not the best partner, the big promotion does not move you closer to your long-held dream, and so it goes.

Just for Fun

Have you delved into taking some steps here, yet await a time to do some introspective work? So often, change is met with resistance. When you change an item's location, do you sometimes forget where you put it? When you concealed a piece of jewelry or some (other) cherished object and then couldn't remember that special spot, what did you do? Know, too, something missing seeks to be found. If it is of value, has a financial or emotional connection, how might you locate it? You have gone through all your pockets, drawers, retraced steps, and still, it does not appear. Now it has been months since it was last seen, and you are beside yourself to find it. What new practice can be introduced here? What practice or procedure can you implement to help locate what is within reach but out of sight?

We have a fun twist for you to engage in if you would like to play in this energy. Consider first how this thing is not missing, per se. It knows exactly where it is. But how can you connect to it again? How can you touch it and feel it in your hands once more? We tell you to release the push/pull energy you have created in your being of not having it or missing it, for surely this works against you. You can try believing you will see it and have found it already, for this is helpful. Yet, is there another solution that might be a bit quicker while allowing you to get into alignment with it? Here it is. A fun exercise to try out.

Sit in a balanced way and clear your mind. Ask for the essence of the missing item to be drawn to you. What do we mean by this? Ask for its energetic flow or resonance to be drawn to you and you to it. So the next time you are in proximity to it, you are drawn with a mental suggestion to tarry. How might this work in other dealings within your life? As a co-creator, what or how can this be put into play in a more expansive way? Ask.

Now ask if you can act as a magnetic tuning fork to locate this missing thing. See it in your mind's eye and ask for its energetic resonance to be felt by you. Since you are familiar with it and it with you, focus on it and feel its energy. See if your familiar feelings can create a polarity of sorts to this object. You can try this out now if you like. Play in this energy for practice as all within the field of possibility can be yours when you focus, align and feel.

And might we ask, when you are given direction, why resist it so? Why is your purpose sometimes so fearfully met (when you are so close to achieving your heart's desire) that you shift gears and go in the opposite direction? Overcome this fear as it is the biggest obstacle for you to achieve the goal of realizing all you seek. Sit now, clear your mind, and just be for a time. A few minutes will suffice. Sit and be now. Focus on your deep breathing and on each breath as you clear your mind.

Do you feel this too complicated, or you don't have the capability to perform an exercise such as this? It's not, and yes, you can. If this were not so, we would not so state. This is something you must be at peace with and practice upon until it feels more natural — play, perhaps, in the wonderment of it.

To practice, sit as you focus upon an object. See if you can visualize where it is right now. Start with something that is not missing, and its approximate location is known. In knowing its relative location, tune in to its vibration. Then move to recognize your vibrational feeling in relation to that item and see if you can detect a subtle energy as you focus upon it. Test what you feel as you move in closer proximity to it. Tune in to feel this energy now. We can work on the subtleties later, but this will give you the gist of the idea.

Or maybe you have kept track of everything in your life, and you don't need to play with this little exercise. Engage with this energy game nonetheless. In this practice, you are working with subtle energy to recognize a familiar vibration as you focus on an object. When you are in its radius, you will feel the object's vibration slightly intensify. All emit a subtle energy and frequency, and because you would be in a constant state of buzz, you do not feel them routinely. At least not until you sharpen your focus through your concentration. This subtle energy has become blended into and exists as a part of your awareness.

When you seek to discern between one frequency and another, you will develop a keener sense here. You will become aware of different vibratory aspects or the resonance found in each thing. Although not as discernible, inanimate objects emit a subtle yet quite distinct energy. The awareness you develop (in time) will assist in your recognition to feel the energy you seek to release, shift, or change.

Chapter 7

Suppressed Emotions,
Predestination and Purpose

We now move to topics we have wanted to discuss for a time. We are here to share these insights in the perfect time to relate them. We hope most, if not all, of these discussions have resonated within your consciousness thus far. Recognize these messages and teachings are imparted in response to insights sought.

We desire for you to find what you have been in search of and for health and healing insights to be perceived and received in the loving manner in which they are given. This was our purpose in joining with another who could put these understandings down into a form that could be communicated and accepted — acceptance based on a level of understanding to satisfy a need existing today.

All life seemingly moves at such an intense speed that finding oneself in the present moment is a near impossibility. Most individuals move quickly to the next task and assignment while connected securely to their technology. Technology was brought forward as a means to help alleviate and expedite processes that had outlived their time. To allow those embodying here to move with less stress and uncertainty. It was also made available to allow more time to focus on those things, which would allow each to feel good — moving away from those unwanted feelings as they move toward better feeling ones. We seek to offer new insights to those who want to experience their best life potential with less strife.

As we seek to offer new insights, so too, today's technology tools open up new vistas to accomplish more in less time. They allow for a more expeditious life to unfold and beneficial outcomes to be realized. However, it seems in the haste of the day, there is yet a reluctance to experience and fully feel life. Sometimes, you feel bad when engaged with certain thought processes, and you realize there must be another way to think or feel. You have a choice. You have an activity, and it doesn't resonate with you. So you find another activity that makes you feel better. One that makes you feel happy and good to be and move in that space. In this way, you can see how you resonate with this, but not with that.

When you enter into an experience you don't like, and it makes you feel bad, do you allow yourself to fully feel that experience and its associated emotions? When you do not want to feel what has been created and such energy becomes suppressed, what then?

Earlier, when the loss of a job was considered, let us add a few details to sweeten the experience. It was the perfect position, in a beautiful setting, and many of the people there were to become lifelong friends. And suddenly, it all evaporated. What happened? Why did things go this way? And when they did, were all or any of the emotions created within the experience felt? Were they felt, or did a stoic-faced person appear who seemingly handled everything as they moved seamlessly through this and onto the next event that moved into view?

Perhaps consider a different scenario. Were you once in a marriage with your soulmate? They were everything you'd asked for in your very detailed request. They fulfilled all of the points you had outlined, but somewhere along the way, they changed … or did you? And when the ideal marriage was no more, what happened? Was the feeling of the loss felt, or was the occurrence pushed through? Did social strategizing develop once the worries and fears kicked in?

Are you yet to feel the deep-seated grief that was created when an all-encompassing loss occurred in your past? Have you paused to allow your grief to bubble up to the surface to be realized? Seek now to fully feel what may have been too painful to do earlier. It is the total and full release of these negatively held emotions that will allow you to experience a more happy and healthy tomorrow. Within these examples, can you see that unacknowledged, emotional energy became suppressed and stored within when they were pushed through during the life experience which created them?

And might we add, when considering any drama from your past, did you take a step back to see how the situation imparted a message? If you saw the message, did it shift your perception of the occurrence? If this did not happen, might you look (back) again? Being less engaged with the emotions created at the time, might you see that component now too?

What results when emotions are not connected to and felt but are instead pushed down and stuffed away? Was the intent to feel them later or to never let them surface again? They certainly seemed too painful for you to feel when they were created. Yet, do you understand why it is necessary to fully engage with them in order to release them? Well, it is this. Their components remain active within your being until you do so. These were very significant happenings, and you cannot get from here to there without taking this part of the equation to heart. For in many ways, there is a breaking of the heart here, and so we discuss this so you might begin to focus more intently when something affects you in such a manner and is so impactful. Do set the intention to revisit such issues to accelerate their release. Do you see how these things are at the energetic core of what we discuss and how they have been further layered upon over time? Other like-kind energy was attracted to this one, and they reside together with those of a similar energetic nature. These things collectively burrow and fester within.

With the passage of time, you've experienced many other such occurrences and stuffed these emotions down too — tucked each of them away. Perhaps not wanting to feel even those lesser ones. Yet all await your connection to them. If not now, when might be a better time? Emotions are layered on and buried together. Can you find where they have been stored and begin to unravel the layers today? If not the deeper issues, perhaps locate the ones that rest on top of those. As we look to do this work, let us consider an alternate way.

REV UP YOUR CELLS

INCREASE IT — TO RELEASE IT

Since all is energy, is it possible to rev up the cells and atoms within your body to so change them that they neutralize any lesser energy that doesn't resonate at the same elevated frequency? Perhaps to frame this as melting away what you seek to release as you engage to energetically clear and clean house. That is what we seek to impart as an option to engage. Consider this premise as you seek to increase the vibration in order to release what has been stored. Do you see?

All is vibrational in nature. Since that is how everything is structured, why not shift the dynamics at play. This is important to note as these culprits are at the beginnings of disease and illness. Do you see that dis-ease is the disintegration of the ease you have experienced within your life? It exists, too, as an alternate way for you to recognize what you could not see without it. When emotional energy becomes trapped in your body, the newly stored frequency is out of alignment with existing energy. So know you can slow, stop or reverse the advancement of degenerative diseases when revamping their operational frequency.

Since disease is a means of course correction in many circumstances, does this recognition stop you in your tracks? So if you have a particular ache or pain, does it cause you to reassess your daily activities or various nuances within your life? Does it cause you to have a new appreciation for those things you took for granted previously? Or even to consider revisiting a former time when you did not have the illness? Well, things would be different if you could do so, right? But each thing came into your life for a purpose. Each experience came to show you something you could not see without stopping to reflect upon it from a different vantage or utilizing another perspective. Now might you see the benefits found in each?

By allowing for pain and illness to be elevated vibrationally and for them to no longer play a part in your world, how were you to know this premise before? How were you to know that pain existed for a unique purpose? Perhaps even to shift you from one way of looking at life as you seek another perspective, in the course correction it offers. To find gratitude for what you were too busy to acknowledge before the illness or pain settled in to become a part of the daily routine. Although this could take a number of pages to explain, the process itself will be rather easy to assimilate. Now as you set intentions that relate to this basic premise, understand the methodology and the fundamentals described here.

YOU ARE A BEING OF LIGHT

YOU ARE MORE SPIRITUAL THAN PHYSICAL

YOU CAME TO EXPERIENCE SOMETHING UNIQUE TO YOU

You are more of a Spiritual Being than your physical form might lead you to believe. It may not seem that way now, but can you see this? Does this resonate as true to you? So with this premise, we look to the understanding that you came to experience something a bit differently from a neighbor, family member, or friend. One experience is not like another, nor is it meant to be.

In that vein of understanding, you may have chosen to experience a certain type of family relationship, achieve objectives through adversity or through support and love. As you look at many who achieve on the stage of life today, you realize they came to experience life from a different circumstance or surrounding than you. It doesn't seem plausible for some who have achieved great things given their status at birth. Can you name individuals who overcame great odds to acquire untold wealth along with an abundant lifestyle, fame, and fortune?

Look around during your conversations as you travel to meet with others. Do you see the totality of their unique qualities? Do you see clearly who your friends and acquaintances are and how they have gotten to where they are today, or do some of their individual paths remain a mystery? The purpose of this question is to confirm so you more readily see how no two experiences are identical. Each is distinct to the one experiencing it. This is so because each sought to experience something unique to them. You can more easily see in a family circumstance, where children are only a few years apart in age, how each one does experience relationships with their parents and life differently than their other siblings. Is this because so much has evolved or changed from one birth to the next, or is it due to differing components or situations sought in another's story?

Although each story doesn't appear on the big screen, do you see each circumstance in a life is but a story? A drama's storyline follows the lead character. Everything that comes into their screen of awareness is about them, even when circumstances seemingly have nothing to do with them. A simple conversation between two friends is somehow seen to be about them as they are the lead in their play. They are the star, and therefore, all must center-around them. Or at least this is as the star of the play would suppose. Thus, this is how the lead in this play of life believes their life exists. All revolves around them and their storyline. They seek to experience wonderful things as they turn the page to enact the next chapter.

Sometimes the script changes. This doesn't happen routinely, but it occurs because of rewrites to the script itself. Certain bit players grumble because they already knew their lines. They don't like how the new storyline is to play out or any script changes impacting their parts. Let's say change is disliked. And so you see this same type of reaction occurs frequently. Many acting upon the stage of life believe they already know who they are playing. They prefer not to reinvent themselves or change their storyline midstream to accommodate another's script changes or their own.

Yet there are others who are eager for change. They move, reinvent, and revel in something more. They are ready for their docudrama to shift, twist, turn, have pages torn out, and even have their script rewritten. They seek the next page to resonate a bit better or perhaps to experience something more to their liking. And so they are in search of their new next chapter since the original script is not what they want now. What about you? Will you welcome change?

So as disease and illness enter in, due to eating patterns, life stresses, or from earlier choices made, some seek a shift to the resulting storyline. They want to find other options rather than those already introduced.

AND WHAT ABOUT THOSE
WHO ARE BORN WITH A DEFORMITY

THOSE WHO LIVE THEIR LIFE WITH SOMETHING
THEY SEEMINGLY DID NOT CREATE

WHAT ABOUT THOSE WHO ENTER WITH
A TERMINAL ILLNESS WHO DO NOT SURVIVE INFANCY

There is also another consideration here. Sometimes individuals step into a role so they can help another feel the effects of their life. If a child passes quickly, how can their premature death be reconciled? Was it for another purpose this child entered into the body? We would say this is so. What gratitude do the parents feel for having experienced any amount of time with them? Each moment is a blessing and cannot be diminished. Did they come to share their precious love for only a brief time? Was their time here to be seen as a gift, rather than from a vantage of loss or grief?

Do you see, however, a storyline can play itself out in a number of ways? It is the same drama, but it can out-picture itself from a hospital bed or from the top of the Swiss Alps. You can come to the realization or awareness in either location and bring that aspect forward. It will depend, however, if you want to experience it from the hospital bed or from a mountaintop. Do you see?

The purpose sought is to experience life. It is perfectly fine to want to experience it from one location or another, from one vantage or another, from in or out of a relationship, with or without certain possessions, with or without certain friends, for all of these things are within the realm of choice. Your personal and unique choices will make the discovery all the more gratifying and worthwhile.

You are the main character in this drama … in your play called life. And what is most important is for you to feel along the way, all of your creations. Life is meant to be experienced from all the vantages that present themselves from choices made. And when you move into the space where you release blockages that exist, then more can flow in and to you. From this vantage, you can align more easily with all you set out to experience, do or be. When engaging from a more effortless posture, all you seek will more readily come into view.

Many of the twists and turns are those of your making. They are the results of your decisions, perceptions, and choices. They are not right or wrong decisions or occurrences, for they are moving you to the next step to stay in step with your storyline. So there are uniquenesses and, although there is a plan, your plan is distinctly yours.

Predestination

What about predestination? This is another component in the mix. There is perhaps predestination in that you have written your play, and you now want to get to the objective of your plan. You imagined it, and now you want to get to the culmination of your outlined steps. So from that perspective, yes, there is a degree of predestination. Yet you must also realize that all is fluid here. Detours line the way because free will choices exist in the path traveled. Your perspectives are uniquely yours, and this is how you see the components that impact your life choices. You chose to experience life from the many vantages that have presented themselves along the way, which is why this life is flavored by those influencing factors.

If you outlined earlier to live a full life here (one of adventure and purpose, while going from a poorer status to a richer one, or conversely, eking out a mere existence after having lived a more lavish lifestyle), these were all choices you wanted to experience so you could understand how something felt. Unless you experience its opposite, it is sometimes difficult to feel the full expanse of the emotion sought. Perhaps you wanted to know what true happiness feels like. To have experienced the joy of your family's love, some loving aspect within a relationship, or perhaps you sought something else. You can be sure of the significance of free will and that your choices are not predetermined. Each selection awaits as you choose the option that's best for you.

Purpose, Passion, Reason for Being

Perhaps you wanted to feel a specific passion, such as joy, or maybe it was more of an emotion that you never quite understood. So you came to express and feel it. This is what you came to project onto the screen of life. In the energy expressed through its emotional equivalent (or in its essence), you sought to bring forward some vibratory component into consciousness. Do you see, your gift is the vibration found in the feeling created as you engage with the focus of your desire. It is evoked vibrationally in the process of creating your creation.

THE VIBRATION YOU CREATE DURING THE CREATION OF YOUR CREATION IS THE PURPOSE YOU SOUGHT TO CREATE

YOUR PURPOSE IS TO CREATE A CERTAIN VIBRATION

And so when you arrive at that thing which moves you to do and be as never before, do you move with it and through your day in an inspired way? Do you accomplish more because your passion has moved you to be in step with Universal flow, so now you never want to leave Its expansive portal? You see, all life works to reinforce what you seek to accomplish. As you move in a more purposeful direction, you will find all life aligning to allow for more to be accomplished. For in this existence, all move together as if there were only this one premise. One in purpose and unified in this one singular objective.

And do you see, the energy created in the process of the doings of this activity, is the vibration you desired to experience here? You wanted to feel and know the energetic component found and felt when in the creation of this thing. What would its energy evoke? And so, this is what was sought. The thing itself is the mere byproduct of the vibrational aspect you wanted to feel through the experience of it. So you see, it is not as you may have believed, as the thing you want to create is vibrational in nature. Something that will always be uniquely yours to know, share and take with you at the conclusion of this life. It is (from this posture) birthed and made real as you express it here.

So it is not a specific tangible thing you sought to bring to Earth and its inhabitants, but rather an energy or vibration. All is energy, as we have said, and so is your unique gift. It is created when you consciously connect with it, bringing a vibrational frequency into this dimension through your doings or actions and releasing that aspect into the world of form as you express it.

**Your purpose is quite simply an
unparalleled feeling, vibration and resonance
you sought to experience and express here.**

Chapter 8

Stored for Your Convenience

If you are creating a vibration rather than a thing, how will stored emotional energy alter what you want to produce? Certainly, one would impact the other. Your personal dynamics would be altered, and a more natural flow would interrupt the sequence in play like a domino effect. Each experience creates its own vibrational equivalent. Each is meant to be felt when created and not stored. Stored vibrational energy could modify or alter what you seek to experience or produce.

Universe knows you want to feel and know each emotion stored because you created them. Connecting to and feeling everything you create is the reason you came here. And yet, you have chosen not to experience certain ones or to limit their expression. So where to put that which has yet to be fully realized while you are in physical form? The intention was to store it close by for easy access. Since your body is your vessel and temple, storage there seemed most fitting. There's plenty of room as it's only energy.

It's so handy to have everything easily stored inside of you. Stored for convenience and readily available when you want to feel each thing you've created. You will surely want to feel each of them since that is why you are here. Universe knows all are here to experience and feel. Your body has been used as a vessel or container, where so many things are accessible. They are all close by, located in one handy place. Unfortunately, sometimes you'd rather not feel this or that emotion but prefer to keep them tucked away.

WHEN EMOTIONS REMAIN IN LONG-TERM STORAGE, HEFTY STORAGE RATES ACCRUE

Have you stumbled upon something in a past activity that produced an experience you didn't like? Nor did you like the associated emotions it produced. Can you just get past this thing and move on? This thing wasn't as you thought it would be, and you've had quite enough of that — whatever that was in this experience. And there were also things that went along with those emotions, and you would rather not experience any of those things either. You didn't want to experience them previously or even now. But why should you choose to focus on all of this today?

Such feelings, you know as emotions, are saved for you to deal with when you are ready for them. And perhaps it might be better to experience all of these creations collectively, for they are yours and yours alone to feel in the manner and time preferred.

Let us share the concept of crying as a child for a greater understanding of what we discuss here. When you were a young child, you experienced something that made you cry. But how were you told to stop crying? Maybe you cried for some minutes, and surely that is enough time to process any emotion adequately, right? Crying as a child and playing out a tantrum when dealing with emotions have such a subtle difference.

But know, it is the vibration of the adult to the child that resonates with the child. To allow a child to free fall with outbursts that go on and on is not healthy for either the child or the adult. So the compassion the adult feels toward the child during those trying times is the greatest means to soothe this energy. And the child will feel this energy, for they are looking for a connection, of sorts, as they acclimate to their new surroundings.

This is especially true for a newborn infant who seeks comfort in their new body and life experience. This is what you might realize as you seek to calm them. Engage with a loving energy as you interact with these little ones, for aren't they seeking to feel the Love they felt before they entered their life here? Now they seek to feel your love and protection as you embrace them. They seek to feel your comfort and empathy.

Trapped emotions are meant to be experienced, even the ones you do not want to feel currently. When you place a lot of focus on anything, this is a signal to Universe to bring you more of that because surely you would not spend a lot of time thinking about those things you do not want to draw in. Why would you? We discuss here emotional energy not yet felt, which remains stored in your body. These await the opportunity to surface and to become known. In this way, they can be expressed and released.

Perhaps you were unaware for the need to feel these things you've created, so you have accumulated them. Each new yet similar emotional vibration attaches to another layered in proximity to it. Each resonating with the original energetic frequency that attracted them to where they now reside. They await your desired connection. Universe doesn't want you to forget about these others, as they are all stored together for easier access. Like-kind energy attracts one to the other and keeps them together in close proximity. So let us get to why you want to feel this stored energy.

Each emotion is energy, vibrational energy. And when this energy is not flowing at the level that resonates in conjunction with your body, when it pushes up against the flow of your body, the resonance or vibration there works in a manner, *not in harmony* with its surroundings. So when you store this type of energy, and you store enough of it, this energy will energetically fester. This is how disease is formed within the body. And if you were able to look at the formation of disease, as do scientists, you would see cells vibrating differently and not in sequence with what surrounds them. As such, they would not be aligned and would work in opposition or in aversion to other cells existing in their proximity.

So in this recognition, do bless each ache and pain and ask what these quirks are trying to tell you. You surely feel the residual effects of what you have created and stored. It's tugging on internal strings to tell you, *Hey, I'm here, and I've got others with me.* Now, how can what is stored be readily accessed and released?

The body expresses things a little differently than Spirit, and so there are consequences that take a toll when emotions are left in the body without being expressed or realized. These are the seeds planted that grow, germinate to take on a totally different shape, form, and purpose as time progresses.

Adding more energy to the core energetic frequency does, in effect, give it more momentum and a boost of sorts. If you are in a situation of angst, and you do not change your energetic connection to the situation, an energetic response is created. The same emotion then continues to be fed as other potential aspects remain in play. The energy which was created becomes suppressed as you push through your day. You are unhappy, but you see no alternative or ability to make changes. Do you then deal with things by putting up with something which makes you feel inordinately unhappy? You do not allow yourself to feel what you are experiencing. Do you believe it would be too much to endure to go through the experience, as well as feeling the occurrence?

Do you see that this is (to a degree) a betrayal of self? Betrayal in that you are asking yourself to stay in a situation that is toxic to your being. You would advise a friend differently, would you not? If you cultivate a negative situation and nurture its growth through garnering similar or other vibrationally compatible energy, doesn't it seem likely more of its energetic kind will be drawn to you? And so, will you need to locate a means to keep such growth under control? And if you are unaware of this occurring in the background of your being in the first place, how are you to deal with this then, when all the while you increase the number of negative things being stored?

You travel to doctors, and they have no explanation for the pain you feel, and so this or that is prescribed to relieve the pain or simply to mask it. But do these drugs get to the root or origination of your issue? How can prescription drugs truly make a difference when you have not addressed the suppressed energy at their root? They are the true origination of the pain.

Ultimately, you must ask yourself to handle what is before you. You have a choice. You can address these things or choose to ignore them. Can you instead consider this a bit differently? Can you allow this bad thing, and the negative energy you perceive, to not affect you? Might this energy, instead, flow over and through you without feeling its effect? Can you not receive it? Get to the other side of the situation, person, or whatever is perceived? Allow the arrows and blows directed your way, to go over you or to be deflected from you without insult or injury?

If you are in a negative situation and you do nothing to change the way you feel about the situation you're in, what will result? An example would be the unhappiness perceived from such an occurrence when pushing through the angst of it without addressing how you look upon it. You do not need to seek a resolution in a confrontational manner. Rather the question is, can you shift the way you perceive this thing so it no longer causes you to feel as it did? Can you allow for a shift in the way you see things and view it all from a different vantage to no longer feel the irritation felt before?

Can you see how the unwanted energy (which came your way) wasn't about you at all? As you reflect again, can you recognize it as merely another's shortcoming? Would this understanding facilitate a quick reassessment of what had come before? Can you now recognize how they were dealing with their own issues? This was always about them, not you. How do new insights change thoughts and reactions to any given occurrence? When you view things differently, everything will shift accordingly.

Do you see the belief you held as the illusionary premise it implied and the delusional thoughts this line of thinking evoked? Now when you interact with this same individual, you enlist a practice to not react and not take personally their mannerisms or actions. You let these things flow over and through you. Do you feel the difference?

YOU CAN ONLY CONTROL
YOUR OWN THOUGHTS AND ACTIONS

If you push your way through any circumstance, rather than seek to find its resolution, you do continue to energetically fuel what is in play. Without reaching a resolution within your own psyche, your energetic connection to it is maintained. You remain vibrationally tied to something you don't like and the domino effect this connection spawns. Realize, too, when you see cancers in existence, there is an energetic component that feeds to grow the cancer as all disease begins from misaligned energy.

Imagine, for example, many people at a retail mall and only a few individuals shopping there, one day, catch a cold. Yet ninety-nine percent of those who were walking around did not catch that same cold virus. They did not get the germ. Some touched things, while others did not; some washed their hands, and so on. So, too, there is a vibrational frequency that causes a certain misaligned aspect to occur that resonates from one individual, more so than from another.

Medical aids, doctors, nurses can all be exposed to a variety of things. Yet they seem to be immune to what others more easily contract. There are infections that spread by touch, and they are more easily contracted by weakened patients with compromised immune systems. Those who pass it on do not routinely catch what is spread. Surely from time to time this will vary. Yet, how can this be?

You see, there is a frequency, as all is energy, vibration, and that which resonates from there. And some who are weakened and in a more susceptible state seem to be a magnet of sorts to attract more of what they do not need or want into their lives. Their energy seemingly draws it to them.

You are always moving in the direction to accomplish your purpose even when this doesn't seem to be the case. We seek for this premise to be understood. Thus, it will feel plausible and felt to be more true by you when you align with its core component. You see, all things are either moving you forward, or you are being refocused and rerouted to the original objective you established so long ago.

There is no need to enter into this without having a bit of fun as you recognize these discoveries are moving you closer to your deeply held intentions. Your intentions are a part of your purpose. Do you see them differently or intertwined? Doesn't one move the other forward once achieved? Your intentions move you toward your purpose in a most expedient manner.

The key is staying in alignment. And with just a little effort, maintain your focus on one activity. Specifically, it is to know where the mind is headed. Monitor its chatter so you can cut it off at the pass. Know, too, there are always those Beings who wait in readiness to assist you. Ask for their intercession. They are most eager to help when you ask to enlist their support.

Does your mind seem to take charge sometimes? And do you wonder about the *little effort* mentioned above? Doesn't it seem like it will always be more than just a little effort to keep tabs on all the goings-on of your mind? Seek to work on this issue of focus and refocus current thoughts to better ones when needed. Do not concern yourself about tomorrow or how things will play out in the future. Look only toward maintaining happier thoughts this day. Will you try this? Play with this premise, if only today.

Make a promise to do so, and then see how you feel at the end of the day. This evening, reassess the results to determine if this activity is worthwhile. If you feel good, maybe better than usual, then consider it worthwhile to engage in this practice again tomorrow.

So monitor the mental activity in play today. Each time mental chatter begins that is not positive, simply notice this, then shift to another more lighthearted or happier thought. Stay centered and remain in the mode of the conscious observer. Listen to what is said and recognize you have the power to engage and grow desired thoughts. In this way, you will move more readily to out-picture that which you outlined before entering this physical dimension.

Chapter 9

Subtle Energy Awaits Within

Clear Out Unwanted Energy

What subtle energy have you not felt that you might now feel? Do you yearn for an awakening, energetic shift to be experienced? As you read and engage with these pages, know they evoke the beginnings of a subtle change. This shift will begin when connection is sought to reveal and expose each subtlety now hidden within. Each unique energetic shift awaits this purposeful connection.

Engage with that Part of you which has donned a robe of mortaldom while experiencing life on this planet. Remember, you are born of God and rightful Heir to all the fruits of this life while residing in this temporary physical form. In this knowledge, the shift begins as your inner journey continues on.

When unwanted energy vibrating at a lower frequency becomes lodged within, you vibrate a bit differently than before. Each person pulsates and emits a different frequency than another. You, in turn, resonate in response to another person's energy at a slightly different level after they enter your field of awareness. Know these subtle shifts cause you to move in a different manner, although unrecognizable at this initial stage.

THE SHIFT HERE IS NOT DISCERNIBLE

SEEK TO KNOW WHAT RESIDES WITHIN YOUR BODY AND REMOVE WHAT YOU DO NOT WANT TO STORE

RETURN TO YOUR ORIGINAL STATE OF BEING AND REMAIN CLEAR

Let us explain. What you think and feel are important ingredients, as they are indicators as to how your life will unfold. Can you recall a situation that caused you pain, anxiety, sadness, or some other great hurt? As discussed earlier, if you sought to suppress the pain you felt, pushed your way through the emotional aspect of it, there's a good chance you have unwanted, negative energy stored within your body.

This energy is oftentimes the beginnings of corresponding aches and pains, which are more readily felt over time as life progresses. You came to this dimension to experience life and all the creations coming from your adventures here. When you chose not to feel something or consciously pushed certain emotions away, their energy became lodged, stored, and trapped within. Know that stored emotional energy are simply energetic creations you chose not to feel at their inception. These stored emotions, in time, feel familiar to you. They never left you and await your desire to reconnect with them.

Storing this energy was not done to offer some cruelty to you, but rather they were kept to allow you the opportunity to connect with them before you depart this life. You have the option to experience and feel that which is stored as they are of your making.

As their creator, each awaits your reconnection. Such energy, known as emotions, were not meant to be suppressed. They were meant to be felt when created, but not from the perspective of victim. When you reflect again upon certain experiences, can you more readily see what was offered then? Might you see them as a compass as these things served to redirect you in some form or fashion?

If you relate more to the role a victim would play, seek yet another perspective — one where a more victorious scenario results from a series of circumstances or past perceived injustice. Release the victim's role. Victimhood serves no one, especially you. When this becomes the central theme within the drama of your life, choose another path, a different interpretation or perspective.

Perhaps something bad happened in your past. Can you choose to release the undesired elements which occurred then and retain the intrinsic components gleaned? Might you find value in the message it sought to impart? How many times must you relive something undesired, as it becomes reignited through the retelling of its story? How long must it continue to play in the mind's eye before you say, *Enough!?* The oppressor has probably moved on and is no longer trapped in the drama produced by this past situation. Will you allow yourself to be set free from the shackles that bind you? The torment and sadness need to be felt and engaged with only briefly, so your life no longer attaches to this thing.

You may know of those who have moved beyond self-imposed limitations ... limitations created from anguish and torment experienced during an earlier chapter in their life. They chose not to let their past define them and relinquished the reins that tied them to what was undesired. A happier future awaits you when old baggage is released. Sit with this and consider it now.

Are you ready to leave the past where it belongs? Will you enlist different alternatives when other options are presented to you? Choose to release what has created trauma within your body and psyche far too long. Engage with these emotions and feel them briefly, as you need to connect with them for only a few minutes, not hours. You will know when you have fully felt the more significant ones as it will feel like a cloud of energy has burst open. Will you consider doing this work? As you move from one emotion to the next while we work together, recognize the release will begin when you resolve for this to be so.

Will you seek to feel briefly each thing you participated in creating … even those things you have knowingly suppressed? You've gone to such great lengths to create certain aspects within your life, while not all were specifically of your choosing. It was the energetic aspect you ultimately sought. And so when certain steps occurred, those which were deemed as missteps, other choices appeared. You were propelled out of one circumstance and into the next because of the flow that moved you into a more desired energetic setting.

Your body is the repository for many things that are yours alone. You know your Soul engages with your body, and so, too, it houses energy of your creation. Seek out any subtle energy which is stored as each awaits your desire to engage there to facilitate its release.

If something isn't pleasant, do you wonder why it must be felt? You've created something, a vibratory equivalence to an occurrence, which is meant, in this physical dimension, to be recognized and felt. When that doesn't occur, the energy becomes stored within you. Over time, as you engaged to produce other things that resonated within a similar vibratory frequency, and those created equated to the other, did you push through those familiar feelings too? And when you chose not to engage and feel them as well, do you see how more energetic baggage was then added to the mix? You've tried to feel some of these undesired things, but they felt bad, and you told yourself you didn't want to feel anything like that again. It is for this reason, you have focused so much time on these things and other dramas that resonate with a similar vibration. You want to make sure you never experience any more of that sort of stuff in the future.

These negative experiences and their associated emotions are the very things you may not want to invite back into your reality, yet more of this energy is drawn to you by your intense focus to keep them away. Energy already created does not go away without assistance. All remain safely stored, residing securely within until you are ready to acknowledge and feel them.

Can you feel where they reside? For example, when someone gives you (and you take on) an energy perceived as being a pain in the neck, well, might these hidden emotions reside in the upper shoulder or neck area? You may already know or sense where such seemingly weighty or dense energy resides. Although it doesn't always work like this, there are correlations to where untapped, unexpressed energy resides within your body.

Could how you feel provide some insights? Do you feel sluggish? Do you enjoy engaging in various activities but don't have the necessary stamina to do so? Are you a heavy or light sleeper? Do you have difficulty falling asleep? Does your mind race and never seem to take a break from its mental banter? Are you happy? Use your answers here to know if you need to do some house cleaning to clear out some unwanted things you didn't intend to store. Might you tune in and ask?

So now, after you've paused, let's begin again. Your life is as a result of your decisions and choices. Reading these words is also a choice. As from earlier days, ideas were formulated, and you moved forward based on perceived options. Were they the only options to consider? As a result, your life is as you see it today. And that is a good thing.

DO YOU RELIVE A PAST EXPERIENCE
AND INTRODUCE DIFFERENT OUTCOMES

The life you experience exists as a result of your choices and focus. Accordingly, you vibrate or resonate in accordance with your continued thoughts and actions. We discussed earlier how you might enlist a preference to think happier thoughts, but do you think other thoughts too? If you also think things that make you feel unhappy, how do you go about minimizing and eliminating those as you cultivate others to replace them? How, too, do you go about stopping those repetitive, negative thoughts that never seem to be too far away?

Start now by observing your thoughts and choose to focus on those things that do not create worry, doubt, or anxiety. So simple in premise, yet sometimes more difficult to maintain and sustain this line of thinking. Remain aware, so you might recognize when ideas enter in to take your happier thoughts off-course. Why is that?

Perhaps you have a recurring thought. This thought represents a situation that reappears often. So often, it becomes almost second-nature to think about it. When you identify with these familiar thought patterns, they become comfortable in their familiarity. These may be more elusive, yet they are not impossible to shake.

RECOGNIZE, FEEL AND RELEASE STORED EMOTIONS

If we were to suggest a method to employ here, it would be to still your mind. When you still the mind, can you tune into your body and locate those areas where bodily issues such as pain and anxiety are lodged? The body feels both pain and anxiety, although each are out-pictured differently from one to the next. One is a physical discomfort while the other is mentally discomforting. Do you see the subtle distinction between the two?

How might any unfelt, subtle, and stored emotional energy become recognized by you? Is there a story you tell yourself that continues to bubble up to the surface? Do you think about this familiar event often? Sometimes you change your response, and the other person changes their response in accordance with your imagined internal dialog. Do you reenact this story repetitively? Is there a way to take this circumstance, recognize the emotions they triggered in order to feel and release them today?

The release occurs when you have felt the emotions after they are fully acknowledged and accepted. You need only allow a few moments for this release to be experienced. If this energy has been with you a while, more time may be needed, over a period of time, as you strip away its many layers. If you feel something unknown pop into play without an attached story, let that rise to the surface too. Then, follow the same steps.

So how might you go about shifting thoughts and, specifically, those you do not like? Change your thinking. Stay aware of what pops into your head. This may be challenging at first. You have to remain cognizant of your mental focus and ongoing thoughts to successfully complete this exercise. And if you have not done this before, it may take a little practice. The good news is it can be done. Again, simply begin by monitoring what you think.

FOCUS HERE, NOT THERE

Do you hold fearful thoughts of your future? Do you find your mind readily shifts from one activity to the next? How hard is it to stay on task or on point with any one topic? Do you find it easier to let your mind flit from this idea to that one, never fully anchored to either of them? If you find this to be the case, your oversight is needed, so thoughts do not shift into the negative what ifs and take you to where you do not want to go. So many things could happen in your future. Why focus on bad scenarios? Turn your focus to happier possibilities.

During the workday, when you place your attention on your job, does something trigger your thoughts back to a recurring personal issue? Or does your work provide you with the angst of your thoughts? Is it there that you must remain somewhat centered and focused so you can get through the day maintaining positive thoughts and objectives?

WHEN YOU SHIFT YOUR THOUGHTS,
YOU CHANGE YOUR ENERGY

Do you strive to stay in a more upbeat mode as sometimes your very surroundings seem to plot for something else? So although you try to push through the energy that surrounds you, maybe instead, surrender. Allow different opportunities to present themselves by releasing your unyielding control. Would you like to put this premise to the test?

Try This Little Exercise

As you begin this next exercise, allow yourself to approach life in a less-structured way. Perhaps surrender a more typical or routine response when others engage and seek input. If this doesn't resonate, just consider implementing a different course of action or reaction to how you would normally respond to another. If you can do this, you will have found the key to successfully perform this little exercise. And might this be a solution? For now you engage with these individuals differently than before.

If you have a strict work ethic and those around you do not, this will allow for a less-structured you to appear. If you have a more easygoing or laissez-faire approach, you may have to adopt a bit more passion at work and show co-workers a new enthusiasm when you engage with them once again.

In each regard, a more playful yet purposeful character might now emerge and engage with their peers. When you change up your standard response to any situation, Universe has more of an ability to orchestrate a different outcome. Whether you have a more or less formal demeanor, you might find new dynamics are able to play out within the current one when you change things up a bit.

Some want to play more in their work environment than others, or vice versa. There is nothing wrong with either scenario. Make work fun. Sometimes, if you lighten and loosen up in your role-playing responses, other potentialities can enter in. Well, all could be in play, so to speak. Such changes can produce far-reaching effects. And so, alter the routine and engage life from a different perspective or vantage. See then, how life will engage with you in return.

In this framework, let go of what you are holding onto ever so tightly. Release control to Universe. Ask for an intercession from your Higher Presence, your Guides, your unseen Entourage, your Support Group, Source. Perhaps a spontaneous interaction with your colleagues is just the answer. Or, conversely, one that is thoughtful and engaged in problem-solving and finding focused solutions. In this seemingly free-formed experiment, new opportunities can present themselves. Before, it may have been difficult for an unscripted interaction to occur when everything followed the original draft and was oh-so predictable.

Perhaps let us focus on the analogy of you acting as the lead character within your play. Each character has a specific role to enact. They are scripted to follow the lead and perform their supporting role. As the main character, all the action revolves around you, your decisions, and choices. Everything in this play is seen through your lens and set of rose-colored glasses. Others have to maintain their various roles and the parts they are to play.

You need antagonists to provide growth opportunities. They allow your good instincts and their related attributes to rise to the surface. Additionally, they allow your good deeds to shine. So when you shake things up a bit, do what is unexpected, then you can change the storyline a bit. And now as these oppositional characters come to play out their roles, will your character grow to do even more remarkable things in contrast? So much more can potentially be allowed to flow in when new dynamics are introduced. Accordingly, new choices can be made to minimize some of your play's twists and turns.

So you see, energy can lighten, and lift when you do. Life can flow and you can achieve your objectives more readily when entering into the flow of life. Through your focus, life will return to you what you believe, think, and feel. It will give you more of what you desire to experience.

HAVE YOU BEEN TOO FOCUSED
ON WHAT YOU DO *not* WANT

Even as you pause now, think about how you wished for something bad not to happen, and then it did. Do you spend too much time anticipating the worst-case scenario only to seemingly attract that very thing to you? When you spent time pondering and agonizing over something you did not want, you actually drew this thing more steadily to you by your consistent and unrelenting focused attention.

Do you also see when you place an intense focus on anything, such unyielding attention sends out signals to Universe to provide you with more of it? Why are you surprised then, when unwanted components appear in your life after figuring out every solution to each problem that might come into your future? The undesired what ifs will manifest when you relentlessly anticipate and analyze each worst-case scenario. They come in response to your line of thinking as Universe believes you want more of these things.

WHEN YOU FIGURE OUT EACH SOLUTION TO EVERY NEGATIVE *WHAT IF*, YOU DRAW THOSE VERY THINGS TO YOU

After having done this, do you proudly proclaim how all the planning paid off as you immediately knew what to do when adversity appeared? Since you worked out every potential pitfall, you focused intently on the very things you did not want to come to pass. And in figuring out each potential solution to every unwanted possibility, you drew more of their vibrational essence to you. Do you see how you called these things into your world? You brought the very components of what you didn't want to your doorstep. You drew those unwanted situations ever closer and invited them into your midst through your focused attention.

Life is as you desire it to be. Your life will out-picture all the things you keep drawing into your immediate awareness. If your focus changes, so can what comes back to you. You see, all life seeks to support you. So are the things you desire arriving at your doorstep or are less desirable things showing up? Realize it is important to be aware of what you spend much of your time focusing upon. Focus only on those things you want more of in this life, so this day unfolds with those desired components instead.

Shift out of negative thoughts into positive contemplations and into what is occurring in the Nowness of this time. This requires a degree of awareness and diligence. Allow your thoughts to change and surrender to other possibilities and probabilities. When you change your focus, new desires will result. This is how a shift occurs. These shifts move you to experience another reality more in keeping with your current focus. Soon you will be experiencing life from a different vantage.

YOU WILL HAVE SHIFTED THE COURSE
OF YOUR PRESENT MOMENT,
WHICH WILL IMPACT HOW YOUR FUTURE PLAYS OUT

WHEN YOUR FOCUS SHIFTS,
YOUR VIBRATION SHIFTS TOO

Bring in energy that vibrates in keeping with your new synergistic flow. Intend to fill the newly vacated space with energy whose frequency is of a light, pristine quality. Change up the flux and flow. Thus when you shift and begin to align with a differently held vibrational frequency, you can fill vacuums and voids created with a more desirable energy. Remember, by shifting into thoughts that hold a preferred outcome, you will more readily let go and stop thinking about those things you do not want as part of your new reality.

Always move into better feeling, happier thoughts. The key is to tap into energy that feels better to you. So in shifting your thoughts, everything will begin to change in relation to them. In that change, what returns back to you will be aligned with your newly held vibration.

Consider incorporating the following understandings and tools if they are not already in your toolkit of awareness as they are important components of what you want to utilize and grow within the processes you undertake to engage.

Visualization: Visualize what you want. As you visualize, see new energy waves being drawn to you. See former, unwanted energy patterns fall away. Picture lesser energy falling like chunks of dirty or darkened snow. As these chunky flakes fall to the ground, see them melt and dissipate … focus and feel.

Meditation: Meditate frequently. Sit in stillness with an open mind. Use meditation time to receive messages given from outside of the mind when stillness exists. Listen to uplifting and elevating sounds or musical compositions. Seek to draw in restorative energy and intuitive insights. Receive what you cannot perceive when the mind races or is otherwise engaged.

Energy Release: Ask in meditation for energetic releases to occur. Now as you release unwanted energy, bring in replacement energy to encircle and fill the newly created void. In releasing these older vibratory patterns, see an infusion occurring within the newly opened area as a more preferred, vibrational energy substancc fills you to complete the release process. Access Love to restore wholeness.

Life has an ebb and flow, as does energy. You have the ability and free will to choose and then craft the frequency that flows into your life as you are its creator. If you do not want what you have created, choose to draw another frequency to you instead. What resonates with you now?

What gives you comfort to live the life you prefer? What is your heart's desire? Start by taking the necessary steps to move or shift energy. It is always within your control to make changes by choosing … differently.

Know all is as it should be and thus is. Your decisions have taken you to where you now reside, and that is a good thing. New options appear, and you choose accordingly.

How to Remove and Clear Out Stuck Energy

So how might you begin to remove what is no longer desired? First, sit in meditation to become centered, then ask. Ask for guidance and to see clearly what you may have missed earlier. Write down what comes into your mind. Are you in a good mental space most of the time? Yet do certain negative issues seem to mentally recur as certain patterns repeat and reappear within your life like a bad habit? Is now the time to get to the bottom of this? As you continue in meditation, let former issues continue to surface. Ask, as you seek to see clearly what is given, as you list these things in your journal or on your laptop. Wait to hear the answers provided. Write them all down.

Sometimes the tendency is to push down uncomfortable feelings, push past them and move on. This work allows you to connect to and feel what has been buried beneath and within. Allow each to be expressed in your physical form. Seek to feel these emotions. They are each merely your own unexpressed energy. Such energy had been unknowingly trapped when not engaged or felt at the time of formation. Once re-engagement occurs through feeling them briefly, ask for their energetic release. Now go to the next emotion, or perhaps you will find a series of like-kind emotions. Write down what you recognize and receive.

As with peeling an onion, all are layered upon. Seek to uncover what is located at the core. It is this core issue that has been nestled deep within. This was the original angst. Reconnect to fully feel this energy once more as you engage there briefly. So go through this process for a time. Allow for this energy to flow through you to activate an energetic release. Otherwise, this misaligned energy will be left vibrationally active and captive within you.

Let each thing surface. Feel them as you let each energy flow through you in activating their energetic release. What unhappy thoughts return? Are they tied to any occurrence in your past or what you hope doesn't continue to repeat in your future? Take this first step as you identify and ultimately remove issues when you feel conflicted. When your focus quickly changes from positive to negative, ask what this push/pull momentum is trying to impart. Or are you engaged with a mind game? Become the investigative sleuth as you remain aware and stay engaged to what is currently in play.

So much is possible through each discovery you uncover. You see, you are a co-creator, and as such, you are creating with Universe a means to process, purge, and release (out of your system) what isn't needed. When left unchecked, such energy might create a bit of havoc in your body. Once energy is buried under other energy, they become layered upon and trapped within. When you know this, take steps to activate their release.

Your body was not intended to indefinitely store such baggage within its boundaries. Seek to release what is now trapped and left to fester. In this way, you heal, reset, restore, renew. Energetically attract more of the things you truly desire, so more of that can grow and flourish.

Patterns

See if you can recognize any repetitious, emotional energy that could be grouped together. Patterns are so key in this process. When you recognize patterns, you can work efficiently through them when you set the intention to do so.

List all associated emotions, then seek to collectively feel and process them in a group release — doing so simultaneously. Were they the same or similar emotions from any one experience to the next? This works best when there are many similar trigger emotions that come up together and share like-kind frequencies.

When many different energetic incidents are layered together, due to similarities in their vibration, a pattern may exist. When you begin to recognize patterns, you can choose to group them together. In this way, you allow for a faster, more comprehensive release to occur. Ask for anything associated with these same energetic patterns and their associated feelings to be released simultaneously as you restore the collective flow. Ask for your body to fully release anything associated with the other. Allow the body to process and release these things in a manner it prefers. Open up to qualify all as you surrender into doing this energy release work.

In reconnecting to unexpressed energy, can you locate where these things reside? Where did they become anchored? Where has this energy been lodged and layered upon? Feel the heaviness of an area that has acted as a repository to hold what you were not yet ready to feel.

Where did they become anchored? Focus to feel where these energy reservoirs are located. All like-kind energy typically becomes lodged and layered together. Might you ask to find their location, or do you already know? Are they located in the abdominal area, in or near the heart, in one or multiple locations? This would be good to know and record on your laptop or in your journal.

NOW RELEASE THIS ENERGY

Focus your attention upon where it has been drawn. Focus and feel for only a brief time. In doing so, you allow your body the opportunity to feel each thing as it was meant to be felt. Are you able to mentally bless this energy, before its release? If not, perhaps feel gratitude that you will be free from its grasp as you seek to release it from your life. Mere minutes are needed to fully engage here, so this energy will not continue to fester within. If left unchecked, these are the beginnings of aches, pain, and other unwanted maladies.

Know you can readily move through this or any other process with some practice. Be sure to tune into the area to see if any residual energy remains lodged. If you feel something more remains, repeat the process.

As you seek to release energetic patterns, your core beliefs will determine the preferred method to engage. In other words, if doing work to release patterns in a group method is not embraced by you or doesn't feel right, then it won't be the best or most effective technique for you to employ. Do what feels right.

First, sit with your journal or laptop computer to note those incidents you have tucked away and internalized. Seek to identify a recurring pattern. Describe what surfaces in enough detail so similarities can be seen as you group them together. Shorten them to bullet points or, however you prefer to abbreviate them. Highlight these and their corresponding aspects. List all experiences which pop up and into view as you seek to identify the emotions that surface. How does each incident make you feel?

Once you have identified a number of related activities that continue to demand your attention, gather more occurrences as they bubble up to the surface. Then gather each point and place them into the first column. This column consists of bulleted incidents you've identified that repeat with a varying cast of characters. When identifying a pattern with distinguishable similarities, place them together within the same bullet point. The second column seeks to identify the emotions evoked or perhaps those awakened in relation to the incident.

For example: Record similar patterns recognized with friends, spouse, romantic partners, and the like ...

Incidents:	Emotional Energy Equivalent:
• Shunned, Made to Feel Ignored, → Treated Rudely	• Shame, Abandonment, Self Criticism, Inadequacy Issues
• Being Sided Against, Tricked →	• Sadness, Despair, Loss of Trust
• Abandoned Friendships, → Forsaken Relationships	• Disgust, Anger, Loneliness, Jilted, Surprise, or Shock
• Used Private Feelings Against, → Dishonesty, Cheated Upon	• Betrayal, Fear, Anger, Frustration, Doubt, Rejection

It's only a matter of discovering this buried treasure and finding a means to let this energy see the light of day. Why do we call this treasure? Aren't things as you see them? Why not see this as an easy method to cut off the roots of illness and disease? Expose these emotional disturbances to keep them from remaining unnoticed and nestled within. If you recognize these things as unrealized, buried treasure to be excavated and experienced before they deteriorate, degrade or pollute your system, isn't that a better option?

Feeling buried emotions, one by one, can be a bit tedious if you see it that way. Choose to be grateful for this work. Release this unrealized energy to avoid creating some significant havoc if left in place and in play. However you decide to do this release work, when you peel away their energetic layers, you will find what is nestled at the core. Seek for its energetic core to become known by you to clear it out too.

Feel Briefly to Release

Allow and feel these emotions as they course through your body. Remember, only a few minutes are needed for them to be fully felt. If you were unable to feel a total release occur using the group method for the patterns you've recognized, consider centering your focus upon what remains. Something that was particularly painful may need some additional attention.

RECOGNIZE, FEEL, RELEASE

Choose to recognize, feel and release whatever you find. Ask Universe to step in to take this unwanted energy from you as you ask for it to be transmuted. Can you shift your focus a bit to find the blessing or gift each sought to impart?

After doing this release work, do you feel a bit lighter? Have you shifted or removed a once heavy burden that energetically weighed upon you? Do you wonder why some have inherent back problems? Well we tell you, when you carry the weight of the world upon your shoulders, you've chosen to take on a burdensome role. This undertaking is unceasing, and from a physical standpoint, this sort of mindset is the source of many deeply-rooted problems.

After realizing emotional issues are at the core of most illnesses, can you look at a malfunctioning condition differently? When these things are recognized as being misaligned energy, which is energy not in alignment with Source Energy, might each ache and pain be viewed from a different perspective?

If we remind how pharmaceutical drugs and certain treatments prescribed only mask the pain yet do not eradicate the root issue, might you enlist the steps outlined here? Consider engaging all practices simultaneously to ascertain a more desired outcome at your next medical appointment. Seek to go after these health concerns in a more purposeful way.

So when you move through this process, give yourself time and breathing space to work through what you've experienced previously. If you're reading this book and you have not gathered up enough life experience to engage in the expedited process, work with each individually. Consider it good news not to have so much history.

This work is truly about feeling the emotions you might have felt at the time they were created but chose to suppress instead. There are other processes devised and so seek out what works best for you. Employ those steps you find helpful. We recommend researching other works if additional investigative insights are needed.

The key here is for you to be able to feel your emotions. If you are able to sit with these things and process them, you are succeeding with the intention to ferret out those things that need to be felt and released. However, you may prefer to develop a more customized approach. Maybe you can discover a more concise method that would work to gather up what has been stored. Then process and eradicate what awaits your focus by employing a customized method to efficiently release these things. See if you can create a recipe that works best for you. The key is to tune in to activate what you might release today.

Some of this may seem challenging. Know that other measures will be introduced shortly for you to test out. Experiment with one process and then another. When the right glue is used to repair, items come together and are restored. A glue for porcelain may not work as well if it is applied to an incompatible substance such as wood. Regain and restore wholeness as you set the intention to become renewed. We want you to have options which address your specific needs and more choices from which to choose. Choose what feels best to you. Apply all insights in the manner vibrationally intended.

Play with the following processes as you seek to determine the best fit. You might find one method resonates more strongly than another. Do as you feel directed. Sit and clear your mind meditatively when you engage these practices.

Looping Memories

How might you remove unpleasant memories that continue to loop into your present moment? Let us describe one such way.

Panoramic View Method: Look at your life as if it were painted onto a vast canvas to be viewed in a panoramic format. See as far back as you can and then move across it to see your life's progression. Do you see any points that give you mental discomfort or anxiety? Seek out occurrences which cause you pain or unhappiness and those you wish to release in this exercise. Is something coming into view?

Place your focus upon this situation. As you recall this thing briefly, mentally and vividly see the occurrence. In time you can move to release other things, but for now, let's continue with just this one objective.

Picture this situation with all of the players who were a part of the scene as everything is pulled, stretched, and lifted off the canvas. Now see the scene transform into tiny bubbles. As you feel the experience, sit with this for a time.

These bubbles grow, expand, and pop when you are ready to release the experience. When you return to this life view, the undesired scene is no longer there.

Do similar scenes spring up and into view with the same cast of characters? Can you see all these scenes simultaneously morph into tiny bubbles that pop as they grow to expand their size? Do you have an inner knowing of what this experience, and others like it, came to show you? If their relevance eludes you, can you surrender what you do not yet know?

Will you allow and see all these things expand and pop as they dissipate and disappear from view? Release what is no longer relevant enough to remain a part of this picture. Now piece together all parts of this view joining together the time before and after the occurrences you've released. See a new version without the former, undesired components present. Now only those things which resonate in a happier way remain pictured there.

Having released what doesn't serve you, move in the fluidity and flow that can exist unimpeded as you scan this panoramic canvas once again. If you see another situation or multiple ones, note them in your laptop or write them down in your journal. When you are ready to continue with this work, follow the same steps outlined above until the desired vista is all that remains.

Some portions of your life story might feel better if there were a rewrite or slight revision made to certain components. Each has served to bring an awareness into view as this was its purpose. Recognize what you could not see before without it. Perhaps you are to become an advocate of some injustice, which you could not do without having known personally the injustice perpetrated in your past.

With the Panoramic View Method, you can also do some light modifications. You can move to restore and bring all back into a greater alignment by invoking Universal Love. When you move Love through-out your being and world during this time, so much more can be.

Take any negative picture from your expansive view and focus upon each aspect. Perhaps collectively feel them in their release. Try out these next exercises, too, so you might safely find, feel and release all that appears before you now.

Funny Bubbles: If a rewrite to your script is needed to stop a repetitive negative loop, consider seeing the images of those who created angst in your past, now grow in size and appear-ance. See them take on a funny-looking, disproportionate shape or morph into a caricature. Watch them expand and pop like bubbles blown in your youth. Can you see these bubbles forming in a comical way? Let them pop and dissipate.

Baby Pictures: Now see yourself as a baby with a smile on your face, then again as a child in your early preschool years. Does any occurrence there negatively come up? Slightly enlarge the memory, focus upon them, feel each and then pop that situation as an iridescent bubble. Continue popping all patterns until you have eliminated each and every unwanted memory. Acknowledge, feel, and then release them. Continue with this process to release each unwanted remembrance that comes into view.

Snapshots: See a situation, person, or experience, specifically those you want to release from your continued focus, as a photo-graphic snapshot. See this snapshot morph a bit as these are special photos. They take images out of focus and distort them in a somewhat playful, humorous way. Maybe add odd clothing or funny accessories into the mix. Now move to feel and release any unwanted recollections which come into your mind. It can be a fun way to focus on less-than-fun occurrences when you release an undesired memory in this way. End this exercise by focusing on those times that feel positive and leave you feeling happy.

If needed, make additional short notes to yourself on your laptop or in your journal. Recall undesired situations as you release them like tiny bubbles cast into the wind. Can you see how the energy takes these odd-shaped bubbles, blows them about until they are no more? These are exercises you can do routinely until your recollections are free of those things that might elicit negative or unhappy memories.

Do you feel a bit clearer as you do this work? Then it is no longer work but a joy to go through this little process. If negative memories persist and repetitively play in the background of your mind, try this out. Create play of something that might otherwise cause anxiety. It's a fun way to release unhappy memories and their associated emotions.

Feel what has remained within. Use these exercises to pull out and dissipate what need not remain. Once felt, you can energetically release your engagement with this energy. Clear out these things so they will no longer exist as trapped emotional baggage. This work is good to do as it will allow for a process to be completed by the body, and a quick-release will result. When you feel the energy associated with a stored emotion, you enable its expression to surface.

Take some time to practice with the more playful processes introduced here. Then pull out your journal to begin to list other incidents that spring into view because, within life, undesirable things happen. Is there a deeply-held situation you continue to engage with mentally? Are you ready to resolve a long-held story?

YOU REACTIVATE THE OCCURRENCE ENERGETICALLY EACH TIME YOU RETELL THE STORY

If you routinely re-engage your thoughts with those that keep you stuck in a past occurrence, might we look there? Did something happen in your past that continues to define you? These memories remain active and alive in your life through your focused attention on them. Let us query some points of consideration.

Who will you be if you no longer mentally engage with this story? If you release this traumatic thing, how might you redefine yourself? Who are you without the constraints this thing imposed? Do such things create voids you do not know how to fill? When released, what would you seek to energetically infuse there? What will you think about if not this? Does this topic impact other relationships or your life in general?

So you must, at some point, make a decision to willingly release your story so you no longer remain tied to it energetically. Do you see how you bind yourself to it when you continually relive the experience? Do you also see each time you retell the story either aloud to another, or more especially in your own mind, you reignite it? You stoke the fires, so to speak, and keep the energy alive. If you want to move past it today, make a commitment to do so now … not by stuffing it deep down, never to acknowledge it again, but by allowing these feelings to surface. Ask for their release so you might be free of their shackles. For this to work, you must be willing to let go of the story as it no longer serves you in any form or fashion.

List all the emotions that relate to this experience on your laptop or in your journal. Follow the same process previously described. Move past this occurrence when you envision severing the cords which bind you. Your desire to do so will make it so.

TRAUMATIC EVENTS CAN BE SHIFTED TOO,
IF YOU DESIRE TO NO LONGER BE
UNDER THEIR CONTROL

If the situation you focus upon presents itself to you with anxiety, consider enlisting assistance. Do you believe in Angels, Spiritual Guides, your Higher Presence, Source? Call upon those you would like to enlist to assist in removing any pockets of unwanted energy to move past your current mental loop. Ask for a release to occur. Remain open to see what has been placed in your path in response to your request for help.

Remember, too, that asking for assistance welcomes unseen Spiritual Beings to intercede on your behalf. Your call allows for their entry into your activities and world. Those Beings of Light you cannot see who watch over to assist you. But they will not interfere in your life unless you invite them in. So invite, greet and welcome those who aspire for your success. Ask them to be a part of your inner circle. They eagerly await your recognition of their presence and will not assist without an invitation to do so.

SEND LOVE INTO YOUR ENTIRE SYSTEM
TO RESTORE THE WHOLENESS AND VIBRANCY
THAT RETREATED FROM VIEW
AND MAY STILL BE HIDDEN

Might a clearing and cleaning out process be enacted, which will also further expand energetic components once engaged? Consider adding music, candles, or perhaps incense as you undertake to clear and heal. Listen softly to whatever resonates appropriately with you. Allow soothing and uplifting sounds and aromas to heighten the experience. Now that you've created a welcoming space of reverence and Love, let us begin.

Feel your heart center open. Visualize its expansion as you amplify its energy. Allow Universal Love and its frequency to connect to all which remains unaddressed. As you do so, feel any remnant energy rise up as if a magnet were pulling each one from where they had been buried, hidden, and nestled within. Extract these now from your body vessel as you look to lighten the burden these things might otherwise impose.

Seek out what has awaited reconnection. Look upon each thing with an unimpassioned eye. See them as you allow a new component to enter into the mix. Allow healing in. Seek to heal from the mental angst and constraints imposed upon your body as it harbors many things.

As you feel each unwanted energy bubble up to the surface, ask your Angels or Higher Presence to remove what awaits. Now is the time to feel and release these things, which are so subtle they might otherwise avoid detection. This energy does not serve you or your physical form. Allow for their release to occur as you recognize and feel any remaining remnants too. Release the reins of control to Universe to unbind what was bound.

Consciously ask your Angels or unseen energetic Spiritual Partners to assist you in removing misaligned energy. These things have been stored for a time, but now is the time to let them go. As you do this work, these nuances will no longer weigh upon you as before. Release them from your world as you feel the lightness of being which remains. Ask, and it shall be so. Be light and free.

As you finish this work, close the portal of the past behind you. You do not need to visit, live or remain there. Know your focus resides in the present. Leave behind all you are able to process at this time.

Now sit and focus upon Universal Love's expansive energy as you engage this energy to immediately fill any vacuum created by this energy work. See this healing energy infuse all as it flows through your body once again. Visualize Universal Love moving throughout those areas as you imbue all with its healing vibration. See the body's whole, and complete restoration occur during this time. Mentally seek out vacated pockets which have been cleared out and await this infusion. Can you see Love's energetic vibration and its expansiveness energize what is in need of a boost?

Feel Love flow in. Know as your focus moves onto other things, there is a resonating frequency that remains to fill and infuse your body with this pure, expansive energy. Re-engage with this frequency whenever you need reinforcement to draw in Universal Love's healing energy. It is an all-healing, energetic frequency accessible to you upon your focused attention.

THERE IS NO LIMITATION UPON HOW YOU WILL INFUSE THESE ENERGETIC VOIDS

SEEK TO DO SO CREATIVELY FROM A VANTAGE OF WHOLENESS AND LOVE

As you visualize now, ask for and see fluffy clouds of energy fill the openings created when doing this work. At its conclusion, you will resonate a bit differently. Your vibrational frequency changes, drawing in and attracting more like-kind energy, giving you more of that.

Consider all methods touched upon here and recognize what works best for you. Do other options come to mind? What resonates with you now? Universe is not limited to solely these methods. You can individually create other means by which you release those energetic patterns. They can be processed by your body instantaneously when you intend it to be so. To say this way or that way is the only way (to do this work) is pure folly. They may work for another, and that is a good thing. When they work for you, well, that is key.

We hope you will reflect upon these points for a time before moving on. As you do so, watch how your life moves away from those self-limiting occurrences. Thus, you will release emotions associated with the past by finally experiencing all you have created and held captive within. Now you are left with better feeling memories to keep you moving forward and in step with all you seek.

How does change play a role here? You see, sometimes there is reluctance to change. The first step is to ask for change to occur. You need to be receptive to embrace what change offers. We see it often and find such strong resistance to change. When an energetic shift is sought and you are on the verge of such an occurrence, why elicit a posture that might block its entry?

INTRODUCE CHANGE AND EMPLOY ITS WONDERFUL NEW BEGINNINGS

Why is change such a fearful enterprise to engage when its very introduction could evoke such wonderful new beginnings? This is very puzzling, but it appears to be a strong indicator of what change portends. It seems the mere mention of change brings up such red flags as to cause a complete shutdown in some. We hope you are more open to what positive things might result when you allow them in. And so if change elicits negative feelings within you, first, research within yourself why this is so … sit in meditation and ask.

What comes forward will surely bring change to you, but in a good way. You must be ready for the answers you seek. Do not begin casually, as this would be a disservice to you. These are big steps to engage. We encourage you to be ready for the change which will surely come.

As you read on, consider the new pathways you might traverse. Try out new options, which present new opportunities as you navigate through this life. This means introducing and welcoming change into the mix. Know that change can be a very good thing.

Light Energy — Energetic Light Frequency

As we move to another topic, we want you to understand Light Energy. As you begin to do this work and process what is to be released, know Light Energy can be engaged for the purpose of transmuting or dissipating dense or sticky energy. So let us explore this a bit and make sure all understand it in the same way.

Light Energy is simply energetic light frequency. You will be working in energy when you intend to release what no longer serves you. Quite simply, trapped energy is meant to be set free. So as you deal in this energy, know this is something Universal law oversees. When you tap into this energy, a quick-release occurs, which is most beneficial.

Emotions are simply frequencies or vibrations that are meant to be experienced and felt. Connect with stored energy once again to eradicate and dislodge it from the body. In doing so, a quick-release can occur. Remember, all is energy. Since energy operates at varied frequencies, work with energy (when there is a choice) which is aligned. As choices abound while residing on this planet — choose to work with that which is aligned and whole.

Aligned energy vibrates at (what some might consider to be) a higher frequency level. Conversely, a lower caliber frequency does not flow in the same manner as that which is considered to be vibrationally attuned. Employ this understanding as you proceed. Seek engagement with the healthy aspect first. Shift all aspects to move in sequence and in confluence with the healthy component as you move to elevate one to the other. Align in this way. Now see and become one with *this* flow as you choose to always align with that which is preferred.

And so as you do this work, and should you be so attuned, you may feel a lesser resonance or lowering of your own vibration when dealing with slower, more dense energy. Should you do energy work on others, you may more readily experience what we discuss here. Know yet the preference is to observe rather than to engage this slower vibrating energy. In doing so, you allow for its release and are not in the engagement of it. In other words, in this way, it will stay separate from you.

This is what energy workers have understood: they cannot get involved to seek or affect an outcome. Successful energy workers have no investment in whether or not their actions affect the change their client seeks. Staying impartial and unimpassioned is key here. By not seeking an outcome of their own intent, they allow energy to move effortlessly, effectively, and in conjunction with Universal flow. They are the facilitators of the flow of energy here.

So this point is very important if you intend to work with others in the release of their trapped, suppressed, or buried energy, which some know as stored emotions. All terms are interchangeable. These releases allow for dramatic things to result in life-changing ways. Seek these changes to occur within your own life first before enlisting to assist others.

Chapter 10

Resonance

We move to more fully discuss resonance and how it impacts your life. What is resonance? As you go through your day, do you feel there is a subtle or distinct vibrancy in the air? Does the day seem to draw you into a flow that already exists? There's something in the mix of each day, which we will call resonance. Look to incorporate some of the concepts discussed thus far into the dynamics of each new day.

HOW DOES THIS DAY RESONATE WITH YOU

Imagine how each day is flowing in a pattern or path. Move in step with it as it unfolds. So often, there is a resistance to what presents itself and you become at odds with aspects of the day rather than in its flow. You might look for this, as it is the essence of the day engaging with you. It has a distinct vibrancy. This is its energetic blueprint or key.

Just as you have a set of fingerprints unique to you, so this day has aspects that make it unlike any other. It has its own special qualities that have aligned as outlined and are defined by its energetic frequency. So be open and allowing as you seek to move into a state of wonder for what the day might offer. Although you may outline details you seek to do within the day, there may be something a bit better Universe has in store that is more in keeping with your next step. Might you qualify each request to put the best possibility into play?

Resonance, and its vibratory patterns, propel the day in a way that moves it in alignment with its flow. It is often unspoken, but you know when you are in the day's flow. It will work with you and you with it. Working in conjunction with the day is so much easier than pushing through encumbering dynamics that can slow your progress.

RESONANCE EXISTS IN ALL ASPECTS WITHIN THE FLOW OF LIFE

Resonance is a vibratory frequency. Each frequency has a residual quality that emits a unique pattern. These patterns distinguish themselves (one from the other) in this way. Such vibrational pulses further define it.

To understand this more fully, let us share an example. Do you feel the resonance from notes composed when you play a song and how the chords resonate? They leave you with the vibrational quality expressed in its melody. As such, we move into resonance with songs and their musical lyrics that can rock your world, but in a different way. As with certain vibrationally inspired music, you can tap into a flow that unlocks another potential to be expressed.

In such compositions, a musical score is played to open up the pathways to allow for a better energetic flow to be experienced. That isn't necessary all the time, yet music can work as another tool to further connections made in healing endeavors. You hear such qualities in a meditational offering when you sit and enter into the matrix of its melody. You seek to slow the mind in connection to something Greater and beyond your physical form, or might we say, in this reconnection with Source.

You do not always seek to have this same sort of ethereal feeling when you are engaged in business dealings, although this is something that would be quite beneficial. So there may be other musical assortments you enjoy listening to throughout the day. You certainly realize differing vibrations from one song to the next. Do you realize the melody, beat, rhythm in a song become absorbed by your body? These and other vibrations flow through you and run through your entire system as your blood does circulate throughout your form. Sound vibrations flow and course through you too. Haven't you ever felt the deep (almost heavy) vibrations made by base pulsations?

And so in music, you find vibratory aspects enter in, leaving a residual quality known as resonance. This energetic imprint remains on the cells it touches with its vibrational pattern and frequency. Your body, which is already projecting a certain vibration, shifts to mirror the new musical melody introduced. Each sound imparts a vibration onto your body as you listen to it play within the background of your day.

You have heard it said and perhaps experienced how the music you listen to can change your mood. It can elevate or, in other cases, diminish a state of mind. In the listening, you have modified, altered, and changed the previously held frequency that operated there before.

Fast-paced music may be fun to hear. Does it rev you up a bit? Know that softer, more soothing music can be used to help slow the heart rate and elevate your being. It can lull you to sleep and calm your jitters as it works to raise your mood if it is of a certain frequency. So look to music to do a number of things as it flows within your body to connect with all of your tissues and organs. Its vibrational touch lingers briefly before leaving a residual resonance behind.

Have you ever thought of music as having such an effect? You may have heard of those who research and study the impact of sound. Healing by sound is not uncommon, or is it? Those who play music at a high volume for any length of time might realize the long-term diminishment such loud music has on their eardrums. They might also consider the effects amplified sound has on the entire body. So what about the mind? How does the repetition of anything affect one as it might the whole?

You may already know about chanting and invocations and how they can play a role in healing the body, and how these can also work to help still the mind. In contrast, how does music played repetitively in the background affect you? It, of course, depends on the beat of the music, the lyrics and the vibration created in the process. This is not to say you cannot listen to all varieties of music. Each imparts a different message, and there can be value in many melodies. Know some sounds can constrain and limit your personal vibratory patterns under repeated exposure to their brasher nature. Sounds are in existence for you as a co-creator, in this life, to experience. You can be a scientist in your own right and make some valid discoveries of your own.

So listen to various radio stations and their musical genre. How do certain melodies make you feel? Do they make you feel happy, excited, nervous, or sad? Do they move you into a place of comfort and peace or something else? After you turn off the radio, sit for a moment. How are you left feeling? How do you resonate now? Do you have a racing heart, maybe an anxiousness? If you are listening to meditative music, are you left in a more euphoric state?

These things are important for you to discern as you consider their overt and covert effects. When you drive around and listen to the radio, there is a subtle effect experienced from passively listening to it. Do you prefer hearing music or do you listen to talk radio?

Let's consider talk radio as our example. It does not matter which slant the commentator has taken, so let us say their position doesn't matter. But comments are postured to engage listeners to their line of thinking. Do they persuade their audience by giving examples that engage or enrage them? Do they use elevated words to invite love, or is the preference to incite anger? Does the radio talk show host get excited? Do they get you excited? You see, many things can change your energy, including talk radio.

DO YOU TUNE IN AND ZONE OUT

Do you turn on the television (TV) when you get home? Does it play in the background? What do you have on TV? How does it shift and move you within the day or at the end of the day? Some are TV addicts and can scarcely function without some background noise playing continually. It's a good idea to do a check on yourself and sort out some of this in your own life. Be mindful. Be present. Some of these distractions allow you to check out for a while. They present you with the means to tune in and zone out. When unintelligible sound exists, gray noise is created. Here you can more easily slip into mind banter that causes you to lose focus on being conscious or present with what's going on around you.

Do you wonder what this has to do with resonance? Well we tell you, all this does create a vibrational mix within you. As you move from one vibratory experience to the next, you adapt. Thus, one's resonance changes as focus changes. This is impactful to your entire system. Consider that it alters all within your form, right down to the cellular level.

Your cells change and shift with the introduction of different stimuli. So much of what your body displays is due to all the different factors you have exposed it to in your daily dealings. Isn't it somewhat miraculous to consider all of the adaptations your body can adjust to as you introduce various components into its midst and into the mix?

Think of it now. You go to the grocery store and smell the aromas of various food samplings offered. Some selections are hot, some cold, some spicy, some sweet, some healthy, and others not so much. You sample a couple of items as your salivary glands react to a spicy dip. Your stomach, digestive system, and the like then work to process and absorb the food you've just tried. Next, you sample some crackers and specialty cheese. Again, your body kicks into motion to accommodate these additional selections.

As you walk around, you hear a song you haven't heard in a while, and it brings up memories of your first date. Your body feels a mental projection of this former situation. You feel a slight tingle as you walk down the next aisle. Now the music suddenly changes to a country-western song. This causes you to bristle as the last time you heard it, a big fight erupted while it played in the background. You feel your body constrict as these thoughts race through your mind once again, as you pick up some juice to put into your grocery cart.

All the while you are in the store, your body and mind are adjusting to new influences spontaneously being offered by your environment. It's now lunchtime, and the music is so loud here, it feels like you're attending a concert of sorts. So, in this experience, as in many others, your body must automatically adjust to unexpected occurrences, sights, and sounds. It's rather miraculous when you think about how your body doesn't need any sort of conscious instruction to do this. All of these influences are being interspersed into your world without missing a beat. You purchased all of your groceries while snacking on select food samplings. And now, you don't even need to stop for lunch.

In this example, you can see how your vibration continually shifts as you move from inside the store back to your car. There you can introduce even more vibrational shifts as you turn on the radio, or maybe it just pops on when you start your car. You are still abuzz from the activity and the many energetic shifts which occurred within the grocery store. It's nice to sit in a quiet car for just a moment. So you turn off the radio and sit quietly, feeling the residual vibrations from your shopping experience. You see, you are still buzzing from all of this. And yes, you resonate differently upon your return.

We interject this understanding so you might become more aware of vibrations and how vibratory patterns exist. They shift easily within a day. As such, you cannot nor would you want to escape these patterns as they move and help you adjust to the mix of activity around you. One song was a reminder of when you went on your first date and made you value your current situation. It caused you to buy certain foods which you plan to cook tonight for dinner. Some of the memories remind you to be more mindful in life and appreciate all that is given. You see, resonance is a residual vibration that shifts you within your day.

Does knowing more about resonance change the way you reflect upon the small things that present themselves to you within your day? When you ask for guidance or insights, do you expect to receive an immediate answer? Do you wait for one?

Do you look to the lyrics in a song playing in the background, or on the radio when seeking answers? Do you look for a synchronistic occurrence? Do you even see the small printed sign, as you walk past it, with a message that reminds you to stay engaged in the present moment? Do you see any of these things or are you too focused in thought and miss the clues which appear all around you?

If Universe or Source wanted to respond to your questions, what would need to occur for you to see them? If not a skywriter, would a six-by-six-foot banner need to appear in front of you to recognize insights given? We tell you the banner may not magically appear before you, and the answer provided may not be as you expect or prefer. Yet might something better still await your discovery when you qualify all you seek?

It is in the small moments when engaged in the present moment that answers will become discernible. That is where the answers to your questions can be found. And you must be present in that moment to recognize and see them for what they are, guideposts to show you the way. Are you going in the right direction, or have you veered off-course? Would a large mile marker come in handy about now to show you where you really are in the scheme of things? Do you see mile markers and signals are more visible along your path when you stay present to look for them?

What about connecting within or using your intuition? Might you seek direction there? Consider, too, when you are going headlong into a situation having sought no inner counsel. What about those times? Is input and course-shifting advice given when not sought? Quite simply, we would say *no*. As we have said, you can only receive insights when you remain open to them. Ask for direction, and know as soon as you are receptive to receive, you can become aware of what has been given. The call allows for interjections and answers to be recognized. If you are satisfied with the status quo of (your) life, what can be added to it if you are not looking for other options? So, too, your expectations are quite important. Expect answers. They are surely there and all about you.

Oftentimes, when far along on your life's journey, you get to a certain point and look up from the treadmill of life and wonder where you are and what has been done or accomplished. Have you finally arrived at that place you have yearned to be? Or are you somewhere else after having gathered many physical things along the way? Do these things quench your thirst, to satisfy that deeper hunger you have held in the core of your being throughout this life? Or do you ache for more? This is what has propelled you to seek something more and might be why you are reading these words now. You seek some innate knowledge that will quench your thirst. This wanting is not coming from your ego, but rather it is from your Presence or Spirit, a Part of you that knows you have not yet satisfied what you came here to do or be. Perhaps to manifest something, as you connect to the vibrational component you seek to manifest. Here we discuss your unique contribution to this time-space continuum and knowing it is yet to come.

You can deaden yourself with all the noise and nonsense that can fill your time even when you know it might be better to become centered in the morning or to align with the resonance of the day. Do liquor or other stimulants take you away from the present moment to deaden yet another part of you? Can such stimulants ever activate what you would want to engage in this wanting? Do certainty or uncertainty grow within these times? It's all good and well to have fun, but at what expense?

So know this. The limitations imposed upon your life provide direction. Each one is introduced so you might recognize whether your current path is bringing you happiness or discontent. Realize as you plunge into this or that activity, a course correction may be needed. Know some activities will take you off a more direct route and leave you ... somewhere in the woods.

You see, life occurrences most certainly have an impact on you. We do not wish to overwhelm but prefer you to know and not live from a state of not knowing. So in this new knowingness, seek to move into a space of certainty. Not to give up having fun or experiencing life, but to live life with more resolve and awareness. How do various experiences affect you? Do they bring you such things as enjoyment, happiness, contentment? For surely, you are here to experience life in a pain-free and happier way.

And more importantly, do you seek to be present in each moment? If you go and do without being aware of what is occurring to and around you, who is living your life if you are not being present there? The experience is still happening, while the awareness and acknowledgment within the moment of its occurrence is missing. So we say, enjoy, recognize, and be aware of what is going on.

Continuing in this vein, how can your daily life be further influenced? What do we mean by this? Life does, in this time, allow you a more unique opportunity than before. Now there are new insights, ideas, and discoveries that can change your world. So we look at the uniquenesses of this day and the time in which you live. The discoveries, inventions, and ease they offer allow for a truly amazing time here. Are some of these benefits on your gratitude list? Yet, sickness and disease still affect many. And, in fact, they sideline countless others who have not yet relinquished their foothold on Earth. We hope to minimize the negative impact of these things.

Many illnesses are the result of stresses created within life. These were perhaps created in a work situation or with family members, especially that which relates to what has been stored within. Various playful methods have been suggested to allow for this energy to be released. Why not engage a method of your choice to lighten your load? Also, know if you find similarities in your midst, look to do those energetic releases collectively. That said, let us continue.

Mirror Image

While there are differences between those who incarnate here, there are also similarities. Those familiar traits connect you to another individual energetically at a deeper level. You recognize these aspects instinctively, even though you may not readily recognize those less flattering ones. Let us say the connection is sometimes hard to identify.

Criticism or blame is then assigned to the one who represents that unseen, less-than-desired characteristic. It is attributed through one's own limited lens as it is so difficult to see a blemish individually, within oneself. This alternate method was devised, as it seems one can more readily identify a flaw in someone else. Thus a potential correction is more evidently perceived in this way.

Do you recall a Bible verse which talked about *seeing a speck in the eye of their brethren while being unable to see the plank within their own eye?* Did you understand its meaning? Yes, criticism is easily attributed to another, and yet that same shortcoming or characteristic is so hard to detect in oneself.

Sometimes certain things are hard to identify and see, except in another person. So from this vantage, can you focus once again to see if you can find any similar traits to those things you've said, done, or perceived in relation to these others? Universe has provided a road map of sorts to help you navigate through your play. To offer a course correction when you recognize the cast has been scripted to show you something you could not see without them.

Sometimes the emotions are so strong you think this person is your most hated enemy. Or maybe they just rub you the wrong way. Yet when you can see them in a different light, as the one who holds the key to break you free from your own limited constructs, might you feel differently toward them?

GIVE YOURSELF TIME

Do you remember an earlier discussion touching on antagonists? In the dynamics of a play, antagonists are those adversarial characters who seem to initiate personal growth to become realized by the main character. Begin to look at those who have acted as antagonists within your own life and note their distinct qualities. Be descriptive in your analysis. What specifically ruffled your feathers to cause you to feel so strongly about them? Think or, better still, write down the points that make you feel as you did or maybe still do. Take out your journal or laptop to note characteristics and those situations where difficulties have been encountered. Once you've done this, do any of their traits look familiar? You may be surprised to see what results when you connect the dots in this way. How did you miss seeing these things before when it seems so apparent now? Do you see a particular characteristic was so well camouflaged in you, it almost missed self-detection? Now keep digging.

Sometimes what another does is in no way reflected in you in its exact form. But might you look at the overall premise instead? Can you see any similarities now? For example, if someone is a liar and you do not like their deeds, you might rebuke the person and their actions. But does this person lie as a means of control, gaining fame or power or whatever is believed to be the overall premise for why they lie? Is the character flaw then about control, gaining power, fame, or the like? Is such control or power sought over others or their circumstance? Is fame secretly relished, but not openly? Although these indiscretions are not as easily seen in oneself, each can more readily be distinguished when attributed and mirrored by another.

Are there people you perceive to be doing distasteful things? Yet are any of their disliked traits assumed because how can you really know for sure what they do? You can only assume many things because you never truly know anything about another person completely or absolutely. You can only know yourself. Do you just believe these things you perceive to be true without actual confirmation or irrefutable knowledge? Did you believe something about them because you needed to see it in yourself? You judged them from your own set of beliefs and perceptions. Yes, rose-colored glasses can be misleading. We advise against making such judgments for the limitations they impose.

ISN'T IT EASIER TO RECOGNIZE NEGATIVE TRAITS IN ANOTHER RATHER THAN TO ACKNOWLEDGE THEM IN ONESELF

YOU CAN RECOGNIZE THEM BECAUSE YOU ALREADY KNOW WHAT TO LOOK FOR

YOU CAN ONLY KNOW YOURSELF

What you see in another is oftentimes what exists, although you may not yet see this, in yourself. How would you recognize their shortcomings if you didn't know what to look for? See them as a gift given to you from on high as these people are helping you to see what you could not recognize without them. These individuals are in your life for growth, as they allow you to remove the very thing you dislike and can so easily see in this way.

Now visualize the activities of your day in your mind's eye. Send Love and gratitude to each thing there as we look at this another way. Can you take it one step further and meet with this one? Before you do, can you shift your energy so this meeting produces a preferred outcome? This would change a difficult situation into a more positive one and energetically shift all players in the process.

Do you see when you are in a situation that continues to throw hardballs your way how these things are being used to redirect you? We mentioned earlier changing things up a bit, allowing for a different set of dynamics to come into play, but what about shifting how things affect you so you no longer feel angst in the situation? Will it mean you can stay in a difficult job or marriage indefinitely? Probably not. But it will make things a bit more tolerable while you work to get to the other side of the experience.

SHIFT YOUR ENERGY, AND THEIR ENERGY WILL SHIFT ACCORDINGLY

You may already realize this energetic work can be done in any proximity. In other words, you needn't meet with anyone personally when you work this way. Your energy can instantaneously reach them whether they are near or far, as their location doesn't matter. Yes, a change between the two of you can occur most readily. Your energy will shift, as will theirs when this self-realization occurs. You see, their energy will change in response to yours as they quickly relinquish their role as your antagonist. Their contribution in your play ends, too, when this dramatic shift allows for a natural resolution to flow in.

Relationships, partnerships, and lives can be altered in amazing ways when these energetic shifts occur. There are many methods you can test out, but a successful outcome will result in shifting the energy between the two of you without a physical meeting. Now, wait and see. When you recognize these characteristics within yourself, you will no longer feel the angst you previously felt toward them. Once recognized, you will see these shortcomings for what they are, and they will no longer affect you as they did. This is how you will know you have removed the *plank* from your own eye. Their perceived flaw may not even exist as you once believed.

As you start to consider your own self-imposed limitations, would this renewed perspective change how you see them? Would it shift your understanding of this drama? Oftentimes these individuals come into your life to show you what you could not see without them. So let us agree in the preference to find and recognize this character flaw. Might you now see value here?

When you see something undesired in another, ask yourself if they are acting as a mirror to you. In this way, they will help you to identify what you could not pinpoint before they entered the scene. You will find this to be true even regarding those individuals with whom you perceive to share no common characteristics. You will find the flaws you perceived in them are quite simply your own traits being mirrored back to you. It's easier to see those lesser qualities in this way. Can you go back again through your detailed list to see this more clearly now?

And why are some personal traits so difficult to observe in oneself, yet so easily recognizable when perceived in another? Certain ones may take more time to recognize. Some individuals may find it takes many years to fully embrace and come to terms with shortcomings identified immediately in someone else.

All initiatives are a work in progress. So know there's nothing wrong with taking some time to come to terms with this. All is shown, discovered, and realized in the right time, the perfect time to receive such insights. Sometimes you just have to be willing to see them. Yet, the majority of unwanted traits will be more easily discerned.

Meditate on the points more difficult to determine by surrendering what you do not readily see. Acquiesce to those things you can't pinpoint. This is a means for your own self-discovery to occur without making actual identification. You can also put it on the shelf for a time to allow it to become more recognizable. Clear your mind to allow other insights to flow in. Can you see what you could not see before?

These individuals are a gift to you as they can affect you as no other. They were able to push your buttons, but what about now? You see, once you've become aware of what was not visible previously, a shift can occur. Your energy will change as you become more consciously aware. From this vantage, you can recognize and release the unwanted trait, activity, or mental construct. This may entail some focus, but it is all about realizing and acknowledging what you couldn't see before as you become more self-aware.

As you engage to do this work, all energy will shift accordingly. You see, another's energy changes in response to yours as you move into this new awareness. Future interactions with them will be different because you are no longer operating at the same energetic level. All will more readily shift to embrace this new you. So might you give Universe your gratitude and thanks for this one person who has been able to show you something you may have missed otherwise? In so doing, you are shifting your energy. Do you see how your frequency changes, and this individual changes in a measured way toward you, accordingly?

There are many accounts where people altered their feelings toward one or another in a process such as this. It doesn't matter where you or they are physically placed since this occurs energetically. It is of little consequence if they are in the same room or on another continent. Energy is unbounded and is able to shift and change without limitation.

As you shift, you move from one vibratory pattern to another. You no longer resonate as before. Now, you've discovered the means to resolve an issue within yourself. Likewise, friends or acquaintances might have an underlying energetic pattern you enjoy being around. In such cases, there is a vibrational match of sorts with this other person. They remind you of yourself in some form or fashion.

So, as various individuals appear in your life, know they embody the different roles necessary within the dynamic components of your play. Some of them show you what you may want to change within your own life as they serve as your mirror. Their actions reflect back to you something you could not see without their recognizable, contributing characteristics coming into play.

And will you forgive and love yourself? Release those self-limiting thought-forms. They do not serve you. Will you acknowledge and move to release this or that trait? Are similar feelings or judgments held yet toward another? Is it time to take a look there too?

It is time to recognize that some have come to show you a characteristic you need not maintain. So take this first step to know that even adversity can be a gift in disguise. Perhaps only this one person can raise the hair on the back of your neck when they enter a room. Isn't it funny how you knew when this one arrived? They have a unique ability to connect to you, to pierce the veil, and reach you at your very core. Yes, they connect in a way of dissatisfaction and frustration, but only they are able to raise such an angst of energy from within. Surely, if your best friend did the very same thing, you wouldn't consider their actions in the same manner. You would dismiss them doing the very same thing.

Why don't you play a bit in the field of possibility to see what impact this has in your life? You will see improvements in your current surroundings as your relative energy will no longer push against the other. So when you engage to change certain dynamics, watch and wait. If these people remain in your immediate proximity, they will no longer affect you as before. You will no longer care in the same way, or perhaps you will not see them around as much. Also, you may find you no longer feel the need to stay in that job or relationship. These individuals will no longer affect you as they once did. After a shift, your needs will change accordingly.

ALL IS RESONATING ENERGY IN FLOW

The interplay and the way emotions come into play, and their corresponding energy impacts all aspects within the day. As you move in life, know all is energy. As frequencies change, there is a resonance that continues to pulsate within. All is in a constant state of motion and flux.

So as we consider this, let us ponder yet another consideration. Can you imagine placing yourself into the role of another character within your play? This would present a bit of an interesting twist to its flow, but what if you were able to assume the chief antagonist's role? How would that change the dynamics underway? Would you take on their persona or would you simply portray this character differently? Would you change their voice, and by this, we mean the way they interject themselves within the drama? Or would you just want to see how you feel to be in their shoes? These are all lofty questions, as they suppose you would know enough about this person and how they would act so you might take on their role.

What if you could step into their shoes, if only to see how you would feel as them? Is there enough information to formulate some sort of script of your own? Why would this be an important consideration? What value could this have within your own play? Well, by changing up the dialog, the exchanges between the characters could certainly alter subsequent scenes. Are there ways to confirm your assumptions? Can you get into alignment with this character enough to understand how this experience would feel from their perspective? What might now occur?

We tell you all of the plotting and planning will not get you to where you would know all the dynamics to accurately portray another. Nor will you know, by this method, what has placed them within your drama. You do not have the life experience or the baggage they carry with them. So, although you think you might enact a different outcome, and most certainly you would, you would not be in the same play. Their unique attributes are not yours. Do you see those things that stick out for you are a trigger for you alone? Although a group mentality may exist here as well, there is an overarching component you are meant to see. And it is this. You are to inherently know that your insights are uniquely yours.

We bring back around a query posed earlier asking you to consider how intuition might play a role here. Do you believe your intuition is telling you *this one is no good*? You ponder this and believe a change from this person to another would be better. A new antagonist would be preferred. All the characters in this newly revised play would be so much happier without this one person. It would change everything. All the unhappy dynamics, due to this one individual, would shift. Things would be so much better without them. But do you see how all of the points you believe stemmed from your intuition *announcing how this one must go... must get out of the story*, isn't as you thought at all? Well, is that really intuition, or is it something else? We suggest this to be ego as opposed to intuition. So remain aware and enlist discernment as to what is what and who is who.

In this docudrama, there are no guesses or considerations that will ferret out the answer as you might suppose. You see, when reflections of you appear in another, and you do not like what you see, you might suppose that intuition is trying to save you from a foe. When in actuality, it is someone separate and aside from you who has entered your drama to help you. To incite and move you as no other.

This one is able to connect with you as only they can do. This special connection allows you to feel and experience things from a more heightened sense. We would say they connect to you in a way unlike any other. To show you what you could so readily suppose in them but could not see within yourself. We hope this resonates with you now, as that is the best way to know if something is true for you. See how this resonates within. We hope you know all is resonating energy in flow. And so it goes.

Do you sense some immediate changes taking place? Do you feel a shift within? Do you see that shifts are already occurring as you take some purposeful steps here? By taking these initial steps, you become more self-aware. You are making choices to act or not (act) in a more conscious way. Your vibrational energy is shifting with this new awareness. It is oh-so-simple in premise, although sometimes more difficult in physical practice. Yet, when you move to implement such changes, you break through illusion and move into a space that more fully resonates with the intentions you established so long ago. As you seek this connection, let us now consider the next step.

Chapter 11

Connection

What does it mean to be connected, and to what and why is connection important? What can connection add to your path as a seeker? Are you not only connected to everything here in this dimension but also to those things you cannot see? What does it mean to be connected as such? As you connect to what is Greater than yourself, do you marvel at the simple complexities of life? All that it portends to relate to you and all that is? And why is connection an important ingredient as you continue on?

As you ponder these questions, do you consider how this will affect your future? Or does all connection already exist, and you just need to align with it? Perhaps what you want to tap into is how to reconnect to Source. To further consider what it would be like to connect to the Whole of Universe and to be in Universal flow.

Do you enlist meditation to connect you to that Higher Part of you when you need reinforcement to enlist a calming presence in your midst? Do you seek alignment to know that Part of you, which is not pushed about by the winds of a storm? Recognize that connection to Source during difficult times takes practice before the storm hits. And so, you will want to work on these connections when you are centered and not embattled. Then when life throws you a curveball, you will be able to easily step into and transcend what comes your way because you will have practiced this before. You will already know how to engage from a more balanced aspect of self and ride through adversity with ease, having figured out the process in calmer times.

All evolves and revolves around this connectedness. We tell you all are connected regardless of the belief that this is or is not so. We seek for there to be a greater understanding to this basic premise. Once this is more fully understood, how would this one understanding change you, the individual, and your existence within the collective mix of the whole?

Let our conversation begin by discussing the fundamental difference between those who prefer to be a part of a group dynamic and individuals who seek to remain separate. In the group setting, each must relinquish a bit of their individuality to meld into more of a group mindset and operate in a dynamic where there is a leader and other participants. The leader may change, but the mix of participants remains somewhat constant.

What about those who do not engage within a group of players and prefer their individuality. These individuals display a uniqueness and an inner strength from an ever-changing set of dynamics. Their attributes are a means of distinction for them. They prefer their individuality, almost a separateness. There is nothing wrong with desiring and residing in either situation. Distinct attributes and their corresponding vibrations exist for each dynamic.

In whichever one you reside, know how you treat one another is key. What you do to another, you do to yourself. Until this understanding is fully recognized and accepted, groups will continue to treat those outside of their social mix as separate from them; not embracing the one as the whole, as self. Why are such strong defensive measures often taken against those who are merely one's own reflection? Why does humanity treat different races and cultures in sometimes brutally different manners? And if you came into this realm to experience life, why are choices made to experience things that result in great sadness? Why not experience only those things which elevate?

As you are around other individuals, do you also seek their acceptance? Do you engage in relationship-building activities? Why do you believe acceptance from others to be so very important anyway? And why do you worry about what others think of you? You know others can judge only from their own limited perspective, as that is their only means and measure to do so. Judgment is what people do. It is done almost instantly and seemingly without fail. Judgment is instinctive.

Thus to be in a space of non-judgment is an atypical occurrence. How is it possible, then, to easily operate in this mode without continually working at it? It seems that practice is key since a more immediate response may move an individual into judgment. Does judging or sizing someone up provide a degree of comfort? Yes, a false sense of security may result. This occurs when someone diminishes another as they become mentally defined, assessed, and further compartmentalized. This often occurs as a quick assessment. Do you want to know this person more in your future and perhaps begin a friendship with them? All is done from a limited perspective as the Judge. Each person judges another utilizing their unique, customized lens. All assessments and judgments made are done with assumptive reasoning.

Most often, assumptions are as they appear; they are assumptive and not to be confused with intuition. Intuition is, many times, used in situations where insights are sought and utilized because of surroundings or circumstance. It is brought around here, so you might recognize the difference and not confuse the two.

We now move to discuss connections, the various levels at play, and your connectedness here as fundamental knowledge and further foundational understandings are given.

Creation — the Beginnings

When the world was initially established, the intent was very simple. Universal Source allowed components of Itself to fragment and form. In this initial creation, Aspects of the Whole were multiplied in numbers. As They divided, They became even smaller components of the Main Essence or Source. So each, although separate, still maintained the quality of the larger Whole. So in going out into manifestation, Each held the matrix of Itself. Each was just a portion of the Whole as an awareness of Its original Source was maintained. As time progressed, Essence wanted to experience … more. In this state of Wholeness, there was no diversity. There was only Oneness.

**SO CREATOR BECOMES THE CREATION
AND DOES THAT WHICH IT DOES BEST —
IT CREATES**

**AS SUCH, THE CREATION IS ALSO CREATOR
AS EACH DID BECOME A CO-CREATOR IN FORM**

So as planets and systems of worlds were created, each experienced creative forces in a manner that was different, in vibrational frequency, from the other. Thus some were created in a more frequency-based modality, while others appeared to be a denser-frequency-in-form. Earth is a three-dimensional field and, as such, is denser than many other modalities. Not to say it is the most or least dense. It is what it is.

So operating in this field of conflict-free, limitless potential, interest spawned and was intensified to discover diversity and differences where so little conflict existed. Push/pull was a concept, but, not unlike many premises, existed in theory rather than in practice. And so, there was interest in these things that did not presently exist — where nothing but beauty and light existed. In this realm, to think of it, was as it was to be. And so it was. So to say that there was interest in drama, really, there was a curiosity of how it was and how it felt to be. Such details did play into the dynamics here. So emotions and feelings were also curiosities. What was this, and how would it feel to have thus and such happen?

You see, too, there are parallel universes and dynamics that are in existence simultaneously. Known only to exist in theory as they have not yet been confirmed in this time-space reality continuum. When so much is at play, and time in the etheric dimension is not as time is on the physical plane, well then, the differences were curiosities. Experiences were sought to be felt and realized.

But when man came here and initially kept the awareness of who he was and who he was a part of, well, there was not the opportunity to be fully engaged with the experience. At that time, discoveries such as love, happiness, joy were desired to be experienced and felt. But to truly understand love, well, what is love without its opposite? What is being right if there is not its opposite? Even though we say there is no right or wrong here, there is a different dynamic in play in the physical dimension.

If there is joy and happiness, what is that except in the realization of it. When you realize the value or measure of each, by not having it in its removal or loss, then having a measure of that again does bring a greater appreciation of it. Then, having this or that (from this premise or understanding), makes each experience, and the feelings associated with them, so much more.

So you see, all were necessary in order to achieve a fuller understanding and to allow a deeper experience to be felt. Without one or the other, the full measure would not be completely understood. During this time, all Awareness was in a whole state. Yet from this state of Wholeness, experiences could not be fully realized, nor felt.

And so, Awareness sought separation from the knowledge which existed for those who embodied. Although they entered with their full, expansive connection to Source, this recollection faded. For when the knowledge had remained throughout the lifetime, there was not the full measure of understanding or feeling of what the experience might impart. And so, although never disconnected, the awareness of the connection slipped away. Thus, the individual was able to experience what life was like and how it felt to do this or that.

In time, religions were established to show right from wrong from a certain perspective. The difficulty here was that sometimes those who were not so highly attuned sought control and power within the hierarchy there. They sought power for their own purposes rather than to have the same intentions focused from a more enlightened perspective.

And why do rules need to exist anyway? Surely Universe will return to the individual what each one does do to the other. He will draw more of it back to himself as Universal law dictates through his own line of thinking. Do rules ever truly govern, or do they create an incentive to figure out how to get around the imaginary boundaries they create? Many see rules as a game where they try to circumvent the newly imposed limitation.

And so, how did other thought-forms come into reality here? Initially, Essence came to experience only those things that were of a similar vibratory nature. Thus, only like-kind vibrations could emanate here. So why were different vibrations created? They were needed to show an opposing component within the mix to more clearly understand the depths and degree of happiness sought. And so the counterpoint was brought forward for a means of distinction.

Without an opposing consideration, who is to say what it means to be truly happy, joyful, and such … for that, you would need a countermeasure to experience the full extent of the emotional energy sought. If you only knew happiness, what comparable experience could you draw from if that were all you knew? And in such limited experiences, you would not have the ability to understand or realize the fuller measure each emotion offers.

Sometimes, too, measures are introduced, so a more global effect is experienced. There is a shift in consciousness when this occurs, and right now, there is such a shift occurring.

Just a short time ago, this sort of teaching would have been much more difficult to openly share, except in secret societies. Now there is a greater acceptance of such truths, but we will say that each must read the words in this and all teachings to see what resonates within the pages of such works. Surely each will know what is true and know the truth when feeling the vibrational frequency of the words as they are engaged and contemplated upon. If the words do not feel right, then either it is not yet the time to receive the teaching, or it is not the right Teacher.

What we mean by this is that truths, Universal or otherwise, are still truths, although they may not arrive in the best time suited for the individual to receive their understandings. Since there is not a right or wrong time to receive them, each is advised to connect to teachings at the time appropriate for them. If they do not resonate for you, then let the words go for now and revisit them at a later time.

So too, words are accepted or not (accepted) by the way the Teacher relates them. It may not be the truth expressed, but rather the manner in which the Communicator expressed the truth. If this is so, then seek another Instructor to enlighten you, one that aligns more with your own vibrational preference.

And, too, sometimes you must question the teacher, and the teaching. There are those who would take you down a path that is of no service except to line the pockets of the one who does plot to deceive. Be mindful and always tune in to what is being said to get an internal read on the frequency emitted.

So, in this world, there are measures which seem to be polar opposites to the other. This is so for a purpose. Without the opposite, how do you know what you have found is what you truly want? You could just be making do with what you have found, believing it is all there is. Your connection to Source, to each other, and to all forms in this physical plane are also you in part and parcel. Know that each has a vibrational frequency, continually moves, and is energetically composed.

All is energy. If there were more of an understanding of the connectivity that exists between all forms here, there would most certainly be more tolerance and compassion at play. Again we will say, what you do to another, you surely do to yourself. Will you now see the significance of these words? As you look again, recognize what may have been missed before. Move to give gratitude as you shift into a space of Love and appreciation. Might you pause now and reflect again?

And do you believe benefits exist in the extreme dramas out-pictured all around you? Extreme living is what we like to call it, as extreme circumstances seem to be at play on the world stage right now. Why is this so? If you took physical form to experience life and the differences presented, is extreme reality what you were seeking? Or does it make distinctions which exist between the two, and associated discernments, go too far?

The answer here is yes and no. Beings did and do come into physical form to experience life and the complexities within life and daily living. They come to experience emotions and the feelings that go along with each emotion at all of the different existing levels at play. Differences do exist, and they can be out-pictured in a way that gives distinction to their differences. Enough difference is needed, though, to see the choices clearly, more evidently.

As to whether or not extreme dramas are more prevalent now, this is not so. Historically, wars, cruelty, violence, and other such activities did exist before. With the advent of more advanced news communications, dramatic situations are promoted around the clock in the media. Good occurrences are often deemed not newsworthy, and so they are not promoted as frequently, except when the situation appears as an exceptional or unique occurrence.

Chapter 12

Intuition and Meditation

Intuition

What is intuition? If you don't seem to have it already, can you develop it? How can it be used in one's life, and why is it important for you to utilize it? Have you asked yourself any of these questions? Have you ever been in a situation where you felt an immediate foreboding or inner admonition? Did you refrain from going somewhere or doing something because you felt, heard, or knew you should listen to the small voice within? These are intuitive feelings you have acknowledged by trusting, what some would call your gut. Perhaps you potentially averted something unpleasant because it did not feel right to you. Well, then, that is your intuition.

Why is intuition important? Intuition offers you unique insights and direction from a Higher Part of you. Sometimes it alerts you to some unseen trappings. Have you ever had the hair raise up on the back of your neck? Did this somehow alert you and cause you to take a more cautious next step? Did you heed this warning of sorts? These are signs and signals communicated to you.

Are they limited to an internal warning system, or could there be other components at play? You've heard of Guardian Angels and Unseen Beings. Could they also play a role as your Protector by helping you to recognize what is unseen and help elicit caution along the way?

Do you know what it means to be intuitive? How could your life be impacted accordingly? To be intuitive means being tuned into another dimension while you simultaneously walk and talk on this planet. Some are born with the means to connect effortlessly to what they cannot tangibly touch, while others seek to achieve this potential and take workshops to strengthen their abilities to engage in this way. It isn't necessary for you to have extreme skills here, but it is helpful to be aware of these things.

Have you ever had a déjà vu encounter or moment? That's when you've never met someone, yet it felt like you already knew them. Or have you been to a new city that seemed oh so familiar, or a restaurant (not a chain), and it felt like you'd been there before? Well, these are people or locations which seemed familiar when they were actually new to you. So what does it mean when this happens?

Have you been to this city in another time, or is there a different explanation? Do you find there's a location you've longed to visit or a school you knew you'd someday attend? And when you got there, it felt as if you were recalling the experience. Yet you've never been to this area, much less to this city before. So are these things coming through portals of time to give you an indicator about the path you outlined before this life began? Surely you've chosen and written most of the big plot points within your play. Yet did everything get enacted as scripted, or did the original outline become laden with various twists and turns as you were rerouted back on course? Although the basic premise just discussed was initiated to create aha moments enabling a degree of realization and a feeling of interconnectedness, we now move to discuss something even more significant. It's called free will.

When free will enters into the equation of life, it can shift your outlined plans. So as you consider the concept of a predestined reality, think between the lines. Recognize your destiny is at the end of the outline. Yet, how do you get there? With the advent of free will, your life may take a variety of twists and turns. We cannot say for sure it will actually occur as originally envisioned, although we can say it will play out as it is to be. It will be as it is. And that you are, right now, exactly where you need to be to accomplish all you desire.

The full measure and impact of free will is not fully recognized. So much can change based on your thoughts, decisions, and actions. They can dramatically change the outcome of your reality. This is not to say that taking another course of action is incorrect, for you are not limited to travel only on one path, in one way. You can travel a pathway on a gravel or paved road, or even embark on a highway to get you to your destination. One course will probably get you where you want to go more quickly than a lesser-developed or more primitive road as you may experience less stops, detours, or dead ends. Delays occur when redoing or revising actions taken as these things add time and slow your travel. There is so much more to take in on the scenic version. Who is to say which is better as you might like this newly introduced experience even more. Surely this is not something anyone can boast about knowing which way is best. Each option has its own uniquenesses, and there are merits with every occurrence.

So you might consider using your intuition as you traverse different pathways to determine what makes sense as you move throughout this life. If you can be given inner guidance and direction, wouldn't that be beneficial? If this gets you where you want to go faster, more directly, wouldn't such insights be a preferred option?

Intuition has begun to be used as a catchphrase without the full understanding of what it really is. In knowing that intuition connects you to a Higher Source, whether that connection exists within or outside of you, do you understand its innate purpose?

It is in this degree of connection that you are able to receive ideas beyond your human knowing. You are being given insights from a Greater Part of you or something which is beyond your current mental awareness. But remember, you are not merely human. You are so much more. You have ingredients that bring a mix of commonalities into consideration. Yes, you have a human form, but you came from a Divine Lineage. Not your ancestral roots. Know rather the heritage you brought into being was from your God Source. And as such, you can do and have the capability to express and be whatever you desire.

So intuition will allow you to connect within and beyond your human aspect to something Greater. To understand this more fully, how do you resonate when you connect to your intuitive nature? If you are unable to access it now, know it can be more fully developed like a muscle. In the flexing of a muscle you see the muscle strengthen, grow, and become more defined. This is also true with intuition. Take part in a workshop to develop and grow your awareness and this ability.

You see, intuition can serve you in many ways. Be aware of the *wisdoms* gained by implementing this level of awareness, as it will aid your efforts. We urge you to learn, discover, and tune into the qualities that exist here. Energetically activate and access those skills when you seek to engage with them.

Might you consider use of this expanded understanding? Utilize it as a tool, especially if additional components add to your present understanding.

Visualization: See mentally (in your mind's eye) this thing you wish to create. See it coming into your life and immediate awareness. Engage your imagination as you mentally focus upon each intrinsic component. Mentally envision your manifestation in picture form as you inwardly affirm it to be present in this reality. In other words, believe it is already here. See this thing often. How does it make you feel to have this thing physically placed? Add feeling to the mix.

So how can you shift your frequency to activate this energetic flow and tune in or expand such skills? Let us try a bit of flexing now. Sit comfortably, allowing energy to flow evenly and easily around and through your body. That is what is meant when you are asked to get into a meditative posture. Do you see if you sit in a manner that constricts the flow, it will be a bit more difficult for things to easily fall into place and for you to get the full value of the experience? It is also good not to be so comfortable that you fall asleep. This can easily happen when you feel so mellow with the experience that you dip below the conscious level and sleep results.

So now position yourself so you can be receptive to what is being offered. Close your eyes and recognize how good your body feels. Even if there are aches and pains, honor how this body serves as a repository for your Soul, your Spiritual Form. Really it is Its formlessness we speak of, but for now, let us say Spiritual Form. Sit receptively to await the next instruction.

As you sit and are receptive, visualize silver glistening strings that connect into your heart. These light frequencies are those aspects that have come to give you insights and are linked to intuition. Intuition is not only an inner sense but also an inherent sense outside your form. In this way, you have the ability and capability to detect what you cannot see. Do you see? So how might you expand and grow this innate awareness?

Expansion occurs when you visualize these heartstrings growing ever so slightly in diameter. See their hairlike structure mature and strengthen to become more as a string in density and shape. So grow a component already attached to you as you strengthen its connection. Some imagine and grow these connections in greater measure than others, but for now, take these first steps.

These heartstrings are connected to Source. As such you are amplifying your ability to connect and intensify your awareness. Grow what you cannot see and strengthen your ability to sense what isn't readily visible (or three-dimensional) on the physical plane. This work is a sensory exercise which will allow you to move into an awareness which can be nurtured and grown over time. It also serves you in many unseen ways that can guard and protect you. But intuition can also provide valuable insights. You might also say this is trusting your gut. When you sense a person is going to be important in your life, or if you seek distance from another, this is also your intuition weighing in.

Begin to enlist insights by calling forth players who will impact your life. Seek for them to be drawn into your immediate awareness as you focus upon them now. Ask to know all wayshowers who might assist you in the discoveries you seek to realize. This is an excellent way to grow and develop relationships as you cultivate your discernment to recognize those who will be a part of your inner circle. Many seek close friendships, but do some have ulterior motives in the mix? As you know, it is necessary to become most discerning. This ability will serve you in all you seek to accomplish.

If you've developed these skills already, you know how handy they can be. They can engage when least expected, popping up and into play before you know it. So much is tied to one's alignment or frequency. You can more easily shift into alignment and work from a greater capacity of knowing and doing when engaged in uplifting activities and elevating endeavors.

Meditation

Now let us move to discuss meditation. Do you meditate? And what is meditation? Do you understand meditation's more foundational purpose? You've heard about this thing called meditation, and maybe you've even sat down to try it a time or two. Maybe it's already a part of your daily routine. Do you understand what meditation offers and why it is so very important to engage in this practice? We say practice on purpose, as meditation does take practice to get you to where it might take you. It will move you out of the banter of the mind and direct you inwardly. It will influence how you see things, allow deeper interpretations to occur, and expand certain understandings, all the while facilitating and enabling a reconnection to Source Energy.

Consider engagement in the meditative process we will describe next. Play in this energy when upcoming exercises are outlined, calling for inner silence and a grounded posture. In doing so, you will utilize concepts that will grow and expand your meditative practice. Further consider adding this expanded understanding to your toolkit of awareness.

Meditation: Start with small amounts of time when you seek to pause mental chatter. Sit erect or in a lotus posture, walk, run, or do any process which will allow stillness and an optimum energetic engagement. Become the Awareness. When thoughts appear (such as checklists or to-do lists): observe, and without judgment … seek to mentally release those things which seem to demand your immediate time and attention. Return to stillness. Connect and focus on your breath and breathing. Seek stillness to strengthen your connection to Source. Practice often.

Do you often reflect upon the premise of your physical form? You are more than the physical body which anchors you to this world. You will certainly see this understanding communicated here. You see, you are more than the fingers and toes which enable you to accomplish so much within the day. But if you do not have all of your digits or all of your other body parts, are you any less than who you were before the loss of these things? Certainly this form does not define you. You are Essence and a part of the Source of all Life. You are a part of the bigger Whole, and in that Wholeness, you have more abilities and capabilities than you may currently realize.

So meditation takes you outside of the mind, outside of its banter, and places you in a space to connect you with your Source. It is from Source Energy that you came here to experience life. Perhaps the full measure of the experience anticipated then isn't as it was conceived. It is denser for sure, but it seems some want to embrace the mental construct: life is hard. And that sort of construct is a part of what we hope to dissipate in the course of this book. With new understandings at play, your mental construct can be whatever you wish it to be. Do you see? You might be holding onto a concept your parents held, or some of your friends believed, or perhaps you heard and embraced this at some point in your past. Maybe you felt it. You experienced that life never seemed to give you a break, and so it felt difficult.

We tell you it need not be so. Life is as you choose it to be. You can focus on the positive rather than the negative, for all is drawn to you by your thoughts. Do you see when you change up your thoughts, you can change your world? And that is what meditation offers. It is and can be used as a reset button of sorts. It will allow you to tap into a space which will re-engage, renew, and reignite your Soul. Thus you can move forward with a refreshed demeanor.

Wouldn't that be a wonderful gift for you to access and employ? In this way, you can go, do and be without any self-limiting thought-forms entering into the mix of your day. Recharge your internal battery like an electric car, which is refueled when plugged into an electrical outlet. It is there that each can find the means to recharge their own battery when they are in need of a boost. Find a means to reconnect to the current that fuels you.

We do Love you, as does Universe. As such, we want your every success and each advancement to be realized. So we let you know meditation, quiet time, prayer are all a means to reconnect you to a Higher Frequency. These will tether and buoy you up when the goings and doings become a challenge. We are not suggesting for you to engage in them only when life has become difficult or as a means of last resort. Anchor now the ability to enter into that space so when your mind races dramatically, when you are under siege mentally, you will automatically be calmed in a space now easily accessible by your past practice. When all life seems to be closing in on you, well, that is a most difficult time to slow the mental chatter enough to start work on reigniting and re-engaging this connection, especially if you have not already established your practice.

There are verses and mantras which can help you more readily slow the mind from its unending banter. One such example was given in our *Little Book to Find Your Purpose*. Consider now deep breathing. This is another method to still and slow the mind. See and feel the difference as you now breathe deeply in and out. Counting 1-2-3, focus upon the breath going in and out. Enlist this measure to become more centered. Be in unison with it.

Deep breathing also offers components to help you establish a connectivity. This connectivity brings desired attributes into fruition. When a more deeply held connection is accessed, new understandings can be more readily gleaned. Otherwise, such insights may be missed or dismissed. So know this is a most worthwhile tool. Make it a point to focus on breathing more deeply when you are present and mindful.

Health components are gained from this process as well. There is a training or retraining, of sorts, which occurs as you engage to breathe deeply. Consider, too, other variations, such as focused breath or conscious breathing. This is where you consciously focus upon each breath as you breathe in and out. This method retards the mental activity in play as you seek to engage in this way. We hope you will play with these and other options to facilitate your spiritual objectives as you make allowances for the outcomes you seek. Meditation and the slowing of the mind are necessary in that they will allow for a connection that will calm, restore balance, and prepare you for the day ahead.

Gratitude and its importance, although previously explored, do play a role here as well. Might you set aside some time within the day to become centered and aligned through gratitude? You will move into the day differently when aligned as such. Do you see when you place your being into alignment with the flow of life, you move more in step and are more purposefully placed? Whether you align through one method or another, know each serves as a gateway to connect you differently than might otherwise be. Establish a consistent pattern of practice.

Might we suggest a meditative posture to employ, which you may find beneficial? Depending on your attunement, sit with your feet uncrossed and placed flat upon the floor. Cup your hands in your lap. The reason for this is you are not crossing energy as you allow for an energetic flow to move throughout your body without it becoming blocked or obstructed. Some do cross their legs and sit in what is called a meditative posture. There are many positions to choose from, so it is only a matter of preference to choose what feels right and does align you in the manner preferred.

Now, clear your mind. If you find mental chatter hard to silence, enlist a method already introduced as you test out processes for practice. What resonates with you now? Take some deep breaths and feel your diaphragm engaged as you breathe. Once you have begun to clear your mind and move into focused breathing, relax further into this practice. Stay with your meditation. When thoughts of various daily activities pop up, or other distractions appear … recognize, observe and release them. Then move back into your meditative practice by employing focused breathing, a short mantra, or another technique to minimize the mind's engagement. Initially, do this for a few minutes. Grow your practice.

Some meditate for hours, and we do not suggest that here. Yet do consistently return at a time that works best for you. If you notice becoming detached from your body as you move into a meditative state, set a soft alarm so you might re-engage with your day as needed. This can be a practice that grows on you as you begin to see and feel the benefits meditation imparts. In time, you will seek to reserve more time for this restorative activity. This may not be the case for others who struggle to maintain a thought-free environment as they grow this ability. Be observant of your mind and, when it wanders, release the thought. Then redirect your efforts back to your meditative practice. It will come together, and your ability will grow.

The Meditation and Intuition Connection

So what does meditation have to do with intuition? You see, one has something to do with the other in that meditation will allow for your intuition to become strengthened and more integral within the day. More specifically, it will increase your day-to-day energetic frequency. It will grow your connection to consciousness. It is a skill you can hone. Thus, it will give you greater awareness, more aha or realization moments, and insights when you operate from a more grounded space. There are some steps you can take to advance this work when you sit and become centered.

Focus on your heart. Feel and tune into your heartbeat. Do you feel its rhythm? Now send your heart and the surrounding area unconditional Love. Send Love from your Expanded Awareness and Higher Consciousness. You know more is in existence than can be seen. Your vibrational frequency will shift as this process grows and expands.

Now incorporate some additional components to further enhance this experience. Start by expanding your focus to send a specially charged, healing energy throughout your body as you seek to align it in pure Love. Engage and align your focus to utilize its expansiveness as this Love resonates at an elevated vibratory level.

Return to your heart center as you sharpen your focus upon that general area. Now take some deep breaths. See your diaphragm move in and out. See your deep breaths become charged with this newly activated, restorative energy. Now move this energy throughout your entire body as all in its path becomes nourished. Fully engage and integrate this energetic elixir with your entire body. See this occurring as you visualize the process we next describe.

Begin at the top of your head, moving down to your toes, and then back up to the top of your head again. Tarry, while at the crown area. As you breathe in, see the head area infused with this healing, restorative energy as you continue to breathe deeply. Allow for a current to begin flowing to the diaphragm as that area rises up with each deep inhalation. Then, as you breathe out, allow for the downward movement of this highly charged oxygen to fill the lower portion of your form. Fill your body and each body part with this pure oxygenated elixir having charged its flow by your intentioned thoughts to do so. See it move upward and throughout your form. Then visualize the return current traveling throughout your body as this energy tarries. Allow it to linger at the head area once again as you continue to consciously breathe.

More was given in our *Little Book* about the deeper meaning of Love and its healing potential. This understanding will be shared again in coming pages, so plan to return, re-engage, and expand the scope of this exercise as you grow the process. In many ways, this is a key of sorts to unlock all you seek. In tuning into this vibrational frequency, you can access so much more.

You see, you are a co-creator of all that touches your life. You have drawn all to you. Sometimes you've asked for things you did not want, as you focused so much time on them. From a state of not knowing, you brought in things you didn't want. So in a more conscious vein, will you now draw into your world what you fully desire?

Call in your Guides. Call to your Higher Self. Call to those who work with you from other dimensions. In so doing, you allow more to become engaged to strive on your behalf. Work can occur behind-the-scenes to propel your desires forward. Be clear and specific. Ask for all Beings who work with you to be centered in Light and Love as you qualify all you seek Universal Source to provide. These things are key as you might always prefer to be surrounded as such.

When enlisting in a meditative practice —

- Ask your Higher Self and those who work with you in other Realms of Light to assist in all you seek.
- Enlist guidance to discern what is most beneficial. Seek to feel their presence.
- Be open to develop new and expanded pathways of purpose.
- Discover all you wish to impart during this lifetime.
- Fully align and believe.
- Seek to clear away what might otherwise hinder your steps.
- Remove resistance blocking what might ordinarily flow easily out and to you.

Some steps may seem small or quite subtle, yet each one does build upon the other. When steps are left out or forgotten, more readily attainable objectives may be harder to achieve. When you remain present, so much more can be recognized, and thus given. And, truly, you can move in unrestricted ways as you release mindsets and engage in activities in a more conscious way.

So as you call enlightened Beings into your midst, ask for recognizable insights to be given too. Have all work in conjunction with your intuitive skills. Be aware of insights as you receive and grow their occurrences through your expanded awareness. Allow not only your Higher Self but also Guardian Angels and the like to engage in your world. Call each in to heighten your sense of knowingness.

Meditation can have a big impact on elevating your mood or frequency. Music and those things you listen to can also raise your frequency. Proper food and diet can elevate your frequency too. But what is the key thing here? Do you need to do an overhaul of your lifestyle choices to be in sync with this so you can get into the flow of it all?

Making good choices is the best way to start. For some, this would be a tweak or two within their daily dealings. For others, this would be a larger objective. So look at your life and take the necessary steps to enact those things that await expansion. A tweak here or there, over time, may be an easier option than making multiple changes simultaneously.

Why not practice moderation in all? Indulgences or excesses block more from entering into your life. You simply have no room for more to enter into the mix. This is especially true when talking about clutter or hoarding. You need to make space to allow for something new to find its way to you. Likewise, when you enjoy a little dessert or a small libation, you enjoy its characteristics but don't throw your body off-center in the process.

We will also say to indulge from time to time is not something that will rock your world. Remember, moderation is key. You are human, and life is meant to be enjoyed, experienced, and engaged. Do not strive for perfection. Work toward another objective. You came from a state of perfection. Here, you can experience life's imperfections, while simultaneously reveling in its bountifulness.

Do you seek also to become centered as you begin the day? In allowing your mind to become still, you can connect to something even Greater than the expansiveness you might currently envision with your outer awareness. Could such a connection impact your life in a way that would be significant enough for you to notice a shift to how you felt before? Will you look for the way your body responds to this activity and any differences which might result? We believe this connection will allow for the greatest of outcomes.

Become centered to assist and strengthen your intuitive skills. As you grow this centeredness, meditation can be engaged more easily. In time, this will prove to be an invaluable resource. Seek a greater connectedness which will allow you to see things a bit differently. What do we mean by this? In this way, you become open to new perspectives. This will allow for a shift to occur in your consciousness. As shifts occur, more opportunities will become visible. Your once limited vantage will open up to new vistas. You will see things and life ... differently.

Centeredness, or to be centered, means to become anchored from a sufficiency felt from within. And so, when life engages unexpected nuances, your footing remains firm. You are not thrown off-balance in what might next cross your path. We will also discuss how to employ a method to engage life from a more expansive yet less emotional perspective. Cumbersome, weighty, or unwanted occurrences from your past can be viewed in a more impersonal, less impassioned, or disinterested manner. One such practice we call the Panoramic View Method, but might grounding be sought first?

Become Grounded

Will you take a moment to sit in stillness to become grounded?

See yourself align by envisioning a pillar of white light stream through your form. See this light begin high above your head as it moves through you and into the center of the Earth. See your body meld into this white light as you see your form elongate into it. Do this for a time. See the light move out into the Earth's center as you would see sturdy and strong roots of a tree project out as this light becomes anchored there. Sit with this for a time. Now feel the energy as it flows through you during this anchoring process. Can you feel an inner ear pulsation as confirmation of this alignment? If not, find some other recognizable sign — as you become grounded.

When you read these things, do you immediately set about to apply your newfound insights or do you squirrel away these treasures and wait to engage them another day? When someone tells you they enjoyed a novel, having found new insights and teachings there, what then? When you locate the teaching, do you rush through it, highlight a few passages, only to place it upon your shelf? Did you even finish reading every page? Did you apply any or just some of the suggestions? Did you garner anything of lasting value from what was written? We can write and discourse all day long, but if you do not apply your newfound knowledge, then it is to no measure.

Thought-Forms

Thought-forms are another means of creation that can be considered along with intuition. We will briefly discuss this now. As you grow your intentions, thought-forms develop and come into play. As thought-forms are created, they move to work in conjunction with your desires. They meld and become one with your intentions. How does this work?

Thought-forms are created when you have a desire you seek to out-picture. As you work with thought-forms, and they begin to have substance and take shape in another dimension, intuition picks up on their presence and works in resonance with these new energetic forms. Thought-forms work in concert, one with the other, to bring you more of what you desire.

Intuition draws to you what you have created from your intentions and gives you access to what is beyond your currently known capabilities. This is more readily recognizable when you actively, consciously engage in the co-creator aspect where you manifest your creation and its energetic blueprint. Thought-forms, then, are manifested energetically to expand and grow your intentions.

Chapter 13

Intentions and Surrender

Intentions with Purpose

How do you intend to bring into manifestation what you desire? How might you generate more of that within your world? What can you do to create your manifestations and materialize your thought-forms sooner rather than later? Why should you monitor, maintain, and update your intentions? Does Universe allow for all the abundance you seek? Can all be enacted and more readily occur when you remain in Universal flow? Or maybe just why are intentions important?

Intentions consist of those things you want to manifest within your life. Do you want to feel happy, enjoy life more, be more prosperous? Will having more abundance, a larger home, a different car, or just having more stuff make you happy? Or, if you are happy after having become centered first, will more material things come into your life? So which comes first, the feelings, or the things?

Do you want to be comfortable in your surroundings? Does that comfort provide you with an inner feeling such as joy, happiness, security, or peace? Do you seek external things because you believe these things will bring you the internal feelings to fill what is currently missing from within?

You sought just the right job so it would bring you the higher income to afford the things that would make you feel more complete and whole. Or maybe you went to a certain college or university as you perceived it would bring you the perfect education. You then conjectured this school would ensure lifelong friends who would allow you to feel a greater camaraderie. These friends would certainly be able to share with you how to be happy and prosperous, right?

So do you believe happiness will arrive when you acquire certain things, or is true happiness ascertained in another way? Do you reason out that buying certain things will get you that feeling? Maybe when you purchase that special car, that incredible house, that island retreat, or take that long-awaited trip, well, surely one of these things will bring you the inner happiness you've been looking for. But did they; do they?

Do things ever bring you to that place of centeredness or contentedness? Once this specific thing has been added to your life, you will need nothing else to feel whole and complete, right? Do you then have the self-satisfaction that all is right in the world? Or is there just one more thing, that if you had that, all would be right in the world? Perhaps if you could move from this house to that one, from this neighborhood to another, if your children were to get into a different school rather than this one, if you were able to take your vacation in a more exclusive location, then you would feel happy and complete. Do you believe this to be so?

Do you see the mind games being played here? For none of this, in the scheme of things, truly matters. As you lie on your deathbed, we tell you none of this matters. You can't take any of these things with you. You've created a lovely existence, and it is surely fine to have all these things. Instead, was your true desire and deeper purpose to feel a certain way inside?

Now might you seek yet another desire? Might it be to ascertain a greater understanding of inner peace, while adding a deeper measure of purpose? Might you move toward this contemplated desire?

You see, as you resonate with a deep inner feeling, it connects you energetically to the comfort and balance you have been seeking. And when you have secured this feeling and have it nestled deep within your core, can you then add other things to it? Now you operate from a different level. Do you see once having established and anchored a certain feeling or frequency (perhaps joy), then the physical things you acquire are merely fun to own? They, however, do not define, nor do you seek them as a means to define. From this reality, the acquiring of things is no longer done from a state of neediness. The things you acquire now add to the joy you have already energetically aligned with … in this reality. Tangible things cannot, nor will they ever, be the thing that would move you into that aligned space. For that, you must shift because this alignment comes in another way. It comes from within.

NOW ALL THAT IS WANTED IS NO LONGER NEEDED

as

ALL THAT WAS NEEDED IS NO LONGER WANTED

For now you are anchored and draw sufficiency from within. Filling a void with more things doesn't ever satisfy that which was sought as a component of self-completion. There is a big distinction in what we have said, for one without the other does not get you there. In other words, having things is not enough. They will never satisfy nor complete you. We say you must be willing to be. And from that state of being, the other components will be so much more. Do you see?

So what might your intention be that would bring more of an inner sense and awareness of self-fulfillment to you? For example, if you were relocating to another home, would it be easier to remodel the home before moving your furniture inside? If the floor plan doesn't flow as you might prefer, would some simple modifications need to occur first, or are some structural ones necessary? Perhaps by removing a wall and some appliances you could open up your new living space.

Does it make sense to have your lovely things moved into your home before you have the guts of your house in place? Otherwise, you must constantly move things around when you add new carpeting, paint the walls, and replace dated fixtures. If there were foundation issues, would you still want the moving trucks to take your valued possessions inside? Would it make sense to do that before getting the foundational things fixed first?

DO YOU SEE MERIT IN HAVING YOUR HOUSE IN ORDER BEFORE ADDING TO IT

Might you get what houses your Spiritual Essence in order too? If you have an unhealthy body, might you do some groundwork to uncover what has been methodically layered upon within? In the home scenario, to limit future cracking and peeling, you needed to remove the old paint before layering another fresh coat on top of what's already there. But shortcuts were taken, and the steps to remove the existing paint did not occur. Now the fresh paint has started to crack, peel and buckle. Layered emotions have the same effect on your body.

Might you remove some undesired things which will allow you to feel at peace, whole, and centered at your core? Take some initial steps and figure out what makes you feel happy and complete as you do the steps outlined here that will shore you up from within. This will allow you to be in a more balanced space, and then you can add more to the equation from a better vantage point.

Just adding things will not sustain your body or that Spiritual Part of you. These things will not provide unbounded happiness forever and ever. To have that, you must be grounded and centered; then, you are at peace. Even when a job is lost, or bad things happen, you remain in a better place because you are in a better space individually.

So if everything were taken away and adversity were to befall you or should world conditions not play out as you prefer, you would still be whole and remain in a more centered state of being as the loss of this or that thing would not destroy you as you no longer self-identify with them. This happens when you no longer seek (inwardly) to be defined through them.

Do you self-identify with the victim? Can you see things through their lens of self-identification in whatever form it has taken? Likewise, do you wish to maintain the love and compassion some past, unre-solved experience brought to your awareness, but relinquish its life-limiting energy? Are you ready to leave it behind as you release what no longer serves you?

Truly, it is not the doings or acquiring of things that will bring you the relief sought. They mask getting in to do the core work, which is what is before you now. We are not saying to have one over the other; rather, consider the ordering. We suggest you choose balance first. Look at what you place your focus upon and the ordering you choose. It is like the cart before the horse. There is a bit of push/pull here as tangible, physical things can provide only temporary satisfaction and can never complete you.

Even relationships seem to depend too much upon bringing another the happiness they desire. Each brings their own centeredness into a relationship. Each is unique and distinct to the other. No one can bring anything to you, and you delude yourself if you believe your happiness is contingent on one or the other. It is up to you and each individual all of the time, in one hundred percent of the way in which happiness comes to serve. No one can provide it. You can't buy it, and it is core work only you can do. You are it. And until you stop to look in the mirror to see what is before you, well, nothing will change until you are ready to face certain components in your life. The dynamics are there awaiting your direction and focus. You see, *all is up to you.*

So we say you can absolutely have whatever you desire. The law of attraction exists, and the abundance it suggests are yours to have in their entirety. But we suggest what you want to attract initially is more than things. You want to bring into your life and manifest a feeling of wholeness, completeness, and centeredness. These things you cannot buy, but you can attract them.

We suggest a little house cleaning first. Might you get your house in order before you seek to bring in too much clutter? More distractions to address will delay work on the foundational issues at your core. We don't suggest this in a negative way, but rather as a fundamental one. We might recommend to not accumulate a lot of stuff first or not to bypass certain initial foundational steps. It need not become complicated. Just go back to the beginning; get back to the basics. If you deal with the first things first issue of you, then the other things will flow much more easily into your life.

So let's do the work of figuring out steps toward setting up intentions which will resonate with you and then you can move toward adding more to the bountifulness that awaits. Are there intentions that could be more fruitful for you to focus on now? Let's see. Do you intend to seek balance, understanding of self, and the clearing away of mental clutter?

When you intend to seek wholeness and firm footing as you become grounded, you anchor and draw in to naturally attract those things you desire. All the while, seek to lessen the ability to unknowingly bring in something unwanted by choosing the thoughts you keep. When you halt for a time the negative flow of energy into your awareness, you open yourself up to other potential aspects in the mix. You will not be working against yourself; rather you will be working toward a direction and purpose unlike any other as you enter into the flow of life. There will not be the push/pull momentum previously in play. You will now be operating from a more simplistic perspective and will no longer be working toward manifesting one thing while attracting another.

We know this sounds counterintuitive, but it is so. When you work from one perspective, but your subconscious works toward another outcome, then you are in neutral. But if both work together in tandem, then everything moves in the same direction. You will accomplish things so much faster when all is aligned and working together. This will more readily propel you toward your heart's desire.

***There is an ordering that must be considered
in order for you to get your intentions
accomplished in the order that will
produce all you seek.***

Ordering is key.

So how do you begin in the best manner to accomplish this initial objective in the shortest amount of time? Actually, once you have these dynamics in place, you may find your wishes and desires change. What you want will grow and further evolve as you shift to see new options and their opportunities. So be open to change your mind. Expect change and engage with new momentums that develop around you. Plan on lots of moving parts.

WHAT ARE INTENTIONS EXCEPT INSTRUCTION
RELEASED TO UNIVERSE TO HELP
IN THEIR ORCHESTRATION

IN OTHER WORDS, YOU'RE ASKING UNIVERSE
TO TAKE THE REINS OF CONTROL
AND PROVIDE DIRECTION

Still the mind if you seek to know elements of the master plan. The plan you devised before stepping into this life. You may not recall it specifically as memory was relinquished, so you might experience this life more fully. Yet you know there is more to this human existence. You know there is more than others are able to see.

A LIMITED REALITY IS ALL MANY INDIVIDUALS
WILL EVER EMBRACE,
RECOGNIZE OR UNDERSTAND

You see, you are here to manifest and bring forward what was outlined before you stepped into this human form. So sometimes you just have to get out of the way to let the actual manifestation occur. As you jumped off the edge to leave the etheric realm behind, and entered into this physical world where you now reside, recall receded. All is illusion in this reality.

So what you believe may not be absolutely so. You see, things may not be as they are perceived. You are not expected to remember what was initially conceived, but you may piece together things and reconnect to their components by feeling your way through this life. Connect to how choices make you feel.

What preferences feel best to you? Do you have a professional aspiration, or do you long for other things? Are you looking for that special relationship? Do your desires seem to flow to you in a more seamless manner as you release the mental trappings that slowed your progress before?

So what might you desire now? Think about it. What would you like to have happen? Might it be to release judgments, love more fully, or feel unending love directed toward yourself and others? As you focus on this now, will you give yourself love as you send a more expansive Love to all parts of your body?

Your intentions work to accomplish a vast array of objectives that assist and lead you to the outcomes you prefer. When making requests to Universe, consider the addition of wording to allow more to enter into the mix queried. Since Universe or Source is connected to the big picture of your life, why not yield to what you do not yet know, could not know currently? Consider again adding language to allow more to enter in. Consider qualifying all requests, so more may be given as you surrender to Universal knowing. Might you again consider adding a caveat to each of your desires? Might you end each request with a qualifying phrase, such as:

... OR UNIVERSE DOES KNOW
HOW THIS MIGHT NOW BEST FLOW
or perhaps
... OR MIGHT UNIVERSE PROVIDE
SOMETHING BETTER STILL

Choose one, the other, or yet another qualifier you devise. These phrases give Universe an opening to fill in the blanks as both allow for more to be provided by Expanded Awareness. Just maybe there is a bigger and better outcome than what you could possibly imagine for yourself right now. Keep it simple. The thinking mind tends to complicate things as it tries to fill in all the blanks. Sometimes you aren't the best one to fill in the missing pieces. Universe can surely offer the best and most expansive outcome.

Do you want to know more about your purpose? We know this often sought question needs to be answered if you've not yet identified it. Do you remember as a child wishing to grow up to become this or be that? Can you remember that line of thinking?

Do you see the attributes of the roles chosen? Say you wanted to become a nun or a stewardess as a child. On the surface, they seem very different, don't they? Yet, what do they both do? They serve. So this is what you might do for a time when you sit down for a meditative moment. As you sit in preparation for a quiet time or other mind stilling session: reflect on what you wanted to be earlier in your youth. Will you take a moment to do this now?

What comes to mind once you've identified some roles? Note them in your journal or on your laptop. If their consistent qualities or similarities are not readily apparent, do some further reflection.

As you prepare for bed each evening, do you present questions you would like to receive answers to as you awaken? Do you ask? So as you begin to do some investigative work on your reason for being, might you implement this simple step … especially if you've not tried it before? Would you try this out tonight and the next several nights? In recalling desired professions from your youth, perhaps ask your Higher Self what these professions have in common. In other words, you saw the connection earlier, as their overarching characteristic is what drew you to want to do that work. Do you see? Otherwise, you would have chosen something that was a more suitable match.

So, maybe right now, your strongest intention is to determine what you had planned to do in this lifetime. What is it you want to do and impart while you are here? Are you doing it already and don't realize it? Start by enacting the small steps outlined above to recall some of the earlier aspirations you held and see if you can recognize if any similarities exist in their scope and purpose. Sit in meditation or pose the question before bed each night until you are able to hear the answer given, as some of this takes a bit of practice.

Your purpose is what makes work seem like anything but that. You could do it all day and all night long without ceasing. You lose track of time and want the day to never end, for you pour yourself into this role, and it becomes a part of you. Have you ever been told to not let your work define you? Well, there is an intersection here where the two do meld to a point of saturation. You become so immersed in the activity as it becomes one with you and you with it. It can become bigger than who you are individually.

Gandhi, Buddha, Jesus continue to teach as they remain great Gurus in this day. Each became individually intertwined with their works. They were one and the same, as they embodied their works. They were inextricably a part of what they sought to bring forward into form. Their attributes are immeasurable as they continue to serve mankind as Luminaries and Wayshowers. And, you see, they did not stop to become someone else or to resume another identity at the end of their workday. They became more, in that they did impart and personify their reason for being all throughout the day and night. There was no differentiation between their work and their Being. Each was synonymously held at all times. So you see, when you find your purpose, it can become larger than life — more than you might ever imagine.

Moreover, who is your mentor, and what do they represent to you? Do they show dedication by their deeds and actions? We know it might seem challenging to connect with Spirit, Higher Self or those Beings who will guide and give you insights when called upon. Yet how might you connect to a sense of your own inner Being, as well as to these others? Is it your intention to enhance such connections? Have you set out to ask for guidance and intercession routinely, or do you enlist assistance only when there is a crisis or specific need to do so?

Would you consider the following questions? When you ask for direction, do you listen, look, and even sleuth out answers? How do you want these answers to be provided? Have you set up a premise or some other parameter for responses to be given? If you do not look for an answer to come to you, how do you suppose you will know when it arrives? The call compels the answer, but how do you remain focused enough to recognize what appears? Have you devised a methodology already, and do you steadily look for each accordingly?

If you look for answers unceasingly, have you determined methods to employ to help you sleuth these things out? Do you sit in meditation and prayer? If so, allow for dialogs pertaining to your question to come into your mind. If you keep shutting off what flows in there by blocking answers when they appear, then it will be impossible to hear the answers given. Distinguish between the small voice when it arrives and the mental egoic voice. Can you tell the difference? Do you seek answers by being given some sort of sign? So if you saw thus and such, it would mean this or that. If so, be alert to the signs which are all about you. Then, watch and wait.

Do you listen for insights within the words of a song on the radio? If you don't routinely tune in, consider flipping on the radio from time to time to see if you hear a message imparted within the lyrics being played. Their insights might incite a greater understanding of what you want to find as each thing reveals something you may have overlooked before. Continually look, stay present, be consciously observant and mindful. When lost in the mind, you can miss these messages.

Surrender

Life progresses, and each lifestream ultimately returns back to Source. Like the ocean is to a wave breaking on the beach, small drops of water remain in the sand until another wave comes; the droplet remains there seemingly alone, separate and isolated. But as the waves roll in and the tide approaches, the droplet rejoins the outgoing tide. The tide re-engages with the droplet as it becomes one with the whole of the ocean. And so it is with humankind, in that each feels separate from Source and seemingly isolated while walking this Earth. But the isolation felt isn't real. Just like the droplet in the sand, all are never truly separated. And when the experience here is finished, and Essence rejoins Source, then each One rejoins the Universal Whole and is complete.

The belief that each lifestream is separate from its Source is not so … as the forgetful component begins shortly after birth. This allows each individual to experience life without a recollection of their Divine Lineage and to more fully experience life here. Not only its ups and downs but also to feel the effects of their life in relation to all they might create in this physical dimension. Yet in the forgetful state, humankind lost the desire to yield some of the components in play back to Source Energy, even though this Source does have a greater awareness of the big picture. As you see, humanity utilizes a more limited vantage, as everything here is fleeting and impermanently held.

In this realization, each might more wisely choose to yield fixed beliefs and understandings. Through limited earthly perspectives, each individual perceives a best course of action that unfolds with many unanticipated twists and turns. Do you see by allowing for an intention to come into being in this reality, and we would say rather to come into this illusionary dimension, there must be a component of wonder and awe in the mix? This component is known as surrender. To dictate anything in a more exacting form is to limit the pure potentiality of what might otherwise exist.

And so the surrender component causes some to pause and wonder how they can get from here to there without some added measure of instruction. The mind and ego are very needy, as they want to be in complete control. Their line of reasoning assumes they hold the greatest solution to each and every what if dilemma. They have plotted out all of the problems which could ever occur, outlining all of the negative ramifications that could take their ambition off-course. But by going through those mental exercises, alternate realities are given fertile ground. Now Universe has been sent multiple requests to satisfy containing mixed messages. These new messages are dominated by those negative what ifs. So now, what else has been placed into cue?

Universe seeks to give more of what is wanted. So when bad scenarios are played continually within the mind's eye, and they come to pass, is vindication felt? Does one exclaim, *Well you see, if I had not thought through all the worst-case scenarios, we wouldn't have been able to employ the solutions so quickly?* But in truth, because they had gone through such mental exercises, these things were called into being as they were drawn into the life experience.

If you do not see this, try a little exercise now. Take something you desire to have that has not been a lifelong obsession or dream. It's a bit easier to draw in what you want when no push/pull energy has already been attached to what is sought. In this way, no limitations have been introduced through oppositional thinking. Focus upon this thing for a minute or two. Now think about all its positive attributes and how these beneficial considerations would enhance your life. Why it would give value to you and your existence. Contemplate on this premise for a few minutes. Release this thought-form to Universe. And now allow some time for its return.

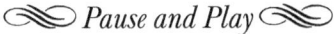

Pause and Play

So, do recognize your intentions are important. With this recognition, only place your focus upon what you want to manifest in this life. If you are wanting one thing, be aware of your continued thoughts, so you don't call forward what you do not want instead. This is often done by reciting or affirming all the reasons why you don't have something, such as: *I never have enough money ... I never get what I want ... I never end up with the right job.*

Try to stay tuned into what you are thinking. Continually observe the thoughts you are thinking and redirect them when conflicting messages appear. Think of the perfect job and why this one position is the best fit for you, then add to each request a qualifying phrase of surrender to open up any alternate opportunities not seen from your current vantage. Remain open to all the positive points that exist, rather than allowing your focus to return to the negative what ifs of life. And then surrender to Universal knowing, as you release any self-limiting thoughts.

Without all components working together in tandem, the outcome you desire may be less than Universe intends them to be. Or you may not see any positive results move into view when mixed messages are sent. Desires when focused in different directions, neutralize requests, and limit preferred manifestations.

Intentions are not to be taken lightly. They are a most valuable component. So right thinking, or thinking which aligns you to what you want, is key. So as you formulate your intentions moving forward, do so from a place of conviction. Know as you align with preferred thoughts (and yes, these are positive), you more readily allow for those desired things to come into being. Always seek to qualify, as you surrender each request … then see if you don't draw in more (to your immediate world) than you ever thought possible.

Practice and play with the energy here. Truly it is most amazing when you can see manifestations take place which were created by your intent. If there were one thing you might employ today to propel you further along in the process, it would be to observe your thinking mind when idle. Were you ever taught to do this? So reframe how you look at things. Seek to always remain aware and conscious of all the thoughts you are thinking. In this way, you might further contemplate, release or engage them.

As certain thoughts arrive that could diminish your achievements today, observe and redirect them. Chuckle and shift your thoughts back to the ones which make you feel happy. Thoughts that make you feel glad to be alive during this time-space continuum. Surely information is now more readily available than in earlier times. And if any component mentioned here does not resonate for you as you might prefer, find other resources available to offer additional insights and answers. We hope to give you new insights as you add some aha moments into the mix of your daily activities. When you see different ways to look at things, transformational changes can take place within your life.

So seek to move and align with this core premise. Know each outcome you desire to achieve is available to you. It is through your intense focus and dedication to what you desire to manifest that clear, straightforward, and unwavering thought-forms go out as requests to

Universe. It is when duplicity arises from dual messages with conflicting intentions that delays result. You will find these dueling messages within the details of those things expressed and the manner in which they are conveyed. This is where you might place your focus and look again. When conflicting requests are provided, a push/pull dynamic is produced. One negates the other. So do check in often with your thoughts and the dialog that continually runs there.

Look at your intentions and see if they are worded in a manner that expresses a uniformity of thought — one that stays consistent in the way you want life to be out-pictured. Know when past patterns are released as you unearth buried treasures known as your emotions, you allow more of the push/pull momentum to be melted away. When thought processes are no longer conflicted, they become more effortlessly aligned.

Truly sometimes, one does work against oneself. This is the self-saboteur: the self-sabotage factor which must be recognized. It is true that when you are unaware of some of the components at play, less consideration is given to the conscious and subconscious dynamics which could be engaged ... conversely. The choices which result may cause rerouted travel and a delay to your journey.

Know that setting an intention can make a big difference too. It is of utmost importance to do so. Intentions alert Universe to your wants and desires. Without a clear path here, all else does not have the necessary momentum to move beyond its current position. A stagnancy results. And so, too, it is best to understand each chapter before progressing to the next.

Know, too, you can be inventive and somewhat creative, as these methods are not the only ways available. You may set up and create your own paradigm in whatever manner resonates with you. The key is to get the momentum and flow going. Isn't that what you want, to move your objectives into Universal flow, so things begin to happen? Then watch the revving up of all the momentum you've set into motion by establishing your intentions. Set them up in a way that Universe understands them with no contradictions or confusion placed in the mix.

Do things flow into your life as you would prefer? Do you continually engage and re-engage with your intentions, or does one brief review of them suffice to let Universe know your preferences? Write down your intentions in your journal, and be sure to date your entries, as they may change a bit over time. You might find it fun to watch and reflect upon all that unfolds as you surrender into this. Remember, too — clarity is what is sought. So play with this a bit.

Intentions — Your Purpose

The Little Book to Find Your Purpose was originally given to help connect those seeking their purpose. We seek to further discuss its premise here. Intentions are those things you want to manifest. So after establishing and connecting to your intentions, you might more easily recognize what has also been termed your reason for being. If defining this objective has yet to be accomplished in your life and its premise has remained undetected, consider implementing the steps outlined within *The Little Book's* pages.

What you've mapped out needn't be spiritual in nature, religious, or the like. Your passion could be to care for the elderly, to raise wonderful children, to perfect the best golf swing, to set up a lovely boutique or even to run an international business. A uniquely held gift only you can expressly create.

Now as you journal your intentions, what might you do to move your purpose into your outer reality? In other words, how might you start to go about implementing and bringing some of this into being? Your gifts can be brought into existence in a way only you can do.

So first, keep them in your immediate awareness as you begin your day. Do you see how you can more easily manifest your desires (known as intentions) when you first establish an inner alignment with Universe? It is in this alignment that you send Universe your preferences. What you want to do, be, and express. Let Universe know, in a nonconflicting way, what you want so more of that can come to you. Do you see? Many times you focus on what is unwanted rather than what you want. Or one premise leads you to discuss the other. This sends out conflicting messages (mixed signals) and so, actually, one cancels out the other and neutralizes your request.

In this same vein of understanding, would asking Universe over and over again for the same thing, in the same way, be good to do? Do you recognize what component is lost in this way? Also, it might not be the best approach were your request to sound or resonate as a demand.

If you choose to reinforce your intentions frequently, do so spontaneously as you feel the words spoken, rather than by merely reciting words. It is in the freshness and spontaneity of the words engaged that Universe can more readily provide what you seek. Your words go out and gather more of their kind. Maintain the essence of your central premise as you engage to feel what is wanted.

Consider use of bullet points as you outline these things in your journal. Jot down keywords to keep them ever-evolving and fresh. Utilize new perspectives to keep them full of energy. Since they are your intentions, you can easily change things up a bit to keep them fresh, vital, and vibrant. In this way, they stay current and are delivered in a manner that does not seem like you demand Universe to hear you.

As you create spontaneous and newly versed statements, more of what you want can enter into the mix. If your intentions become a rote statement or something more mechanical, then you will lose the feeling associated with your words. It is your emotional attachment to the descriptive words which will enable your creation to manifest more quickly. A vibration is created when you feel the excitement expressed through the words you've chosen. Select those words which create a vibrancy and buoyancy to what is sought. It will allow what you desire to bubble up and can be likened to a cresting wave on the ocean's current.

So stay in anticipation and remain excited about what is wanted. Keep the points new and allow this energy to build within you. Feel your creation. Remember to keep excitement, anticipation, and awe in the mix. Awe in the wonderment of it all, anticipation for your expectation of what will be and excitement in that you know it is already here. You will want to feel as if it has already been physically manifested. This will feel more true or real as you grow more aligned with its creation.

It may not seem so initially, but this truth will grow as you more fully align with your words. It will become easier and more believable as you grow into your new reality. Thus, it rings more true to you as you step into this knowing. Your vibration will shift as you express your intentions. You will expand and mirror the vibrational frequency when you begin to resonate with your aligned intentions.

You know your dreams and desires. You also know such desires will adjust and change each day, if only just slightly. So tweak your intentions. You can change things, too, by writing them out in more detail. Expand upon the bulleted points. Feel your words as you see your dreams already existing within your current day. The more you picture or envision this new thing in existence, the more quickly this reality will come into being.

You can have short and long-term intentions. Keep them forward leaning in your frontal lobe thinking. Engage with them at the same time as your daily meditations and when you give gratitude. As you begin your day, you are allowing the day's flow to become activated in and through you as you also align with your intentions. Now release your intentions to Universe by surrendering all points as you allow Universe to complete its missing details. Universe knows the other parts and will add them into the mix if you will but ask.

So release your intentions by allowing something greater to be presented back to you from this All-Knowing portal of expansive and limitless Love. Your intention is not to place restrictions here; it is to allow all that might be to come into complete manifestation. Sometimes you cannot see the allness of what you want. So now surrender.

AND UPON THIS SURRENDER,
MOVE INTO UNIVERSAL FLOW

IT WILL TAKE YOU WHERE YOU WANT TO GO FASTER
THAN YOU MIGHT EVER IMAGINE

From this vantage, what does it mean to surrender? It means to release anxiousness, anxiety, and neediness. This means you allow Universe to work to return back what you have vibrationally set into motion. Now expect to see its full 360-degree return to you. Surrender also means recognizing you may not have asked for something in a way that might best resonate with Universe. It is an acknowledging and allowing that Universe may change things up a bit. In a manner of speaking, you release control over and around the situation. Control around a time frame or a specific way it can come to pass, control around who might be within the dynamic of this return and when it may take place. Remember to qualify all requests.

Some might prefer a streamlined version of this process. Many have been working to this end throughout their lives, maybe not doing it in this exact way, but preferring to expedite the process. So is it possible to introduce another way to do this work that does not take as much time and can achieve a more immediate result?

IF YOU ARE ABLE TO CONNECT TO YOUR INTENTIONS WITH SUCH DEDICATION AND DEVOTION …

DO NOT SLIP INTO A SPACE OF DOUBT OR DISCONNECT, STAY IN A STATE OF ANTICIPATION AND EXPECTANCY,
then
THIS PROCESS CAN BE EXPEDITED

So within your intentions, how might health and healing enter into the mix? Might one of your intentions be to heal and restore your physical form of this or that ailment? Or to relieve some ache or pain? It is important to have a basic understanding of Universal laws and the existence of these fundamental teachings first. In other words, when fundamental points are understood prior to contemplating new beliefs, new understandings can be more readily accepted. Thus, foundational footing is recommended before entering uncharted waters. This allows for an expanded realization to be more quickly adopted as more details become known.

We have written about vibrational frequency here and spoken about how these frequencies resonate within you and all life. All of this world is energy. And so we seek to delve into what is at the root of creation. To think in more concrete terms (even though concrete itself is just a different form of energy). All energy is in a state of constant motion, and in that motion, it vibrates and changes how it out-pictures itself from one form to the next.

Many profess this to be the densest of planets, and there are many other such claims. Yet we tell you, all of this is illusion. Consider if life, and all connected within this realm, were not as they were imagined to be. You see, planet Earth is solely and completely energy in its most base form. All the chatter and associated beliefs are immaterial, for Earth is ultimately energy. This energy has taken on a rapidly moving, illusionary form. Thus, it appears to be what it is not. Some discuss time travel, parallel universes, and alternate realities which do concurrently exist.

And truly, there is no time as this, too, is illusionary. It is that you came to experience life here because it is the place where you have the ability to feel. Thus, it is this characteristic, the ability to feel, that allows for greater self-expression to occur. And that is the reason for its perceived density. The components that complete the equation of existence here allow feelings and emotions to exist simultaneously. Were this not so, emotions would not, could not exist as they do. You see, without form and the aspects that are perceived as heavy, weighted, dense, there would not be the same ability to feel the emotions which are so freely available to each inhabitant here.

Some have said Earth is a schoolroom, and from certain levels of understanding, this is so. Some have said Earth has received Souls from other planetary systems, and that is true, as well. Just as America takes in the many who seek to live here, those from other systems and worlds come here too. All come to experience the perceived density that allows them to feel what they create. These energetic creations are also known as emotions.

So you see, feelings are experienced here in a more significant way. And that differentiates this planet from other systems and worlds, as many other systems operate from a fully dimensional or more vibrational platform. Truly all is vibration from energy. This is so, and don't you know or feel this to be true? Then why do those who incarnate here work so hard to not feel their emotions and actually seek to suppress them?

Do you believe that life experience is the sole reason for you to have embodied? It is true that you have selected your purpose and chosen certain experiences to occur during this lifetime before you incarnated. And it is also true that you need not accept past life karma as it was not intended for you to do so. Yet, if you prefer to balance each and everything you have previously created, it is your free-will-privilege and right to do so. Know, too, perceptions held of what an incarnation is going to be like and how it will be does shift. It is not as perhaps, previously anticipated.

Might you incorporate some fundamental understandings … so you can further build and expand upon such knowledge?

Conception and Birth

Birth is an exciting and much-anticipated occurrence. At conception, a baby cannot speak, and so they are unable to lay claim or communicate to what is remembered. This is also a time of transition for this newborn. They can enjoy the wonderment of their new form. How it feels and how they feel to be here. Surely they feel their mother's love if that was their intention. Or perhaps they feel the security a home can provide unless they were born into a different circumstance to experience something else.

So, as this baby grows and loses the awareness they entered in with, they acquire certain realizations formulated in prebirth and earlier times. The beliefs of their parent(s) or guardian(s), surroundings, environment may also lay claim to influencing the trajectory this life will take as interpretations and perceptions will be accordingly gleaned, understood, and engaged.

Their initial knowledge of coming from another realm, the different vibrational qualities, or other remembrances are routinely lost as time progresses following their birth. And so, this baby is taken from being an expansive, unbounded Soul and is now left in this little body with a more limited awareness. They are rather small and helpless. This reduced stature is an adjustment, and thus, a shift occurs. Memory of their original Spiritual Nature, in time, recedes. And all that remains, for most, is limited to the self-awareness held within their little body. And so this Soul, that once soared without boundary or limitation, now resides in a more confined physical form that has yet to learn how to walk and talk in their new surroundings.

What about things such as conversations which take place around these small ones? Do the words used confuse them, or is the speech engaged too difficult to understand? During the transition time and depending on when the Soul energetically attaches to their form in the womb, the words may be hard to hear or decipher. But, most certainly, the vibration and resonance of the words permeate and infiltrate the psyche of this infant. This little one enters with an awareness and understanding of the intent of the words used by the vibration created from what was said and the manner in which the words were communicated.

Although they may not be able to fully understand the words per se, they do conceptualize what was intended from the impact of the words uttered. They can feel if there is love in the household for them or others. They can sense the vibrations moving forward within their proximity.

These are their somewhat limited, early understandings. They resonate and can respond to loving thoughts and feelings directed to them even as they grow within. As when in the womb, this little one does, in many cases, have a vibrational understanding of what is going on outside of their cocoon-based reality as they grow and evolve during this time.

We say this because when a Soul attaches to its form is individually unique. There is no set time for this occurrence to take place. Is the mother encountering love, support, acceptance, or something else? Is loving touch and uplifting language in the mix, or is it another, lesser vibration being conveyed? Is entry into this life to be a joyous time, or might a different vibrational measure be sought?

Know, too, in addition to recognizing what is conveyed through innate abilities such as what sensory perception allows, the subconscious also works during this time, and throughout one's life, to relate the necessary components gathered then stored, to assist in guarding, protecting and even guiding a lifestream.

A child feels the intent of the words spoken by another through the vibration they emanate, while the subconscious gathers to store information. Such information is gathered, beginning at preconception, continuing on into childhood, and is active throughout one's life. The components gathered and stored there are considered to be pertinent to one's evolution. It works as a silent partner in a field of uncertainty. The subconscious gathers and stores this information as it seeks to help assimilate what is harmful or helpful. It elicits support to the lifestream by moving them closer toward their personally held intentions. It also utilizes the information stored to locate more of those things it seeks to experience or to move away from others as it works in tandem with Universe.

This background information will assist with our discussions as points of clarity to minimize push/pull energy which might otherwise become engaged. We provide this fundamental information to give you a foundational platform of knowledge as we proceed.

❦ Please stop and reread these words ❦
if you need to more fully integrate with them

Seek now to integrate new understandings, so insights can shift and expand how things might be perceived and received. This will enable you to go, do, and be as never before. This is especially true as we seek to impart how to attract and bring Universal Love into your daily living. Yes, this one understanding allows for a shift in consciousness to come into being. This is the time. And we were excited to also discuss this understanding in our *Little Book.* Might you re-engage with this vibrational frequency and incorporate it into your everyday activities?

Think, too, now about the power of attracting as Universal law portends. Recognize the workings here to be similar, yet a bit different. You do not need to continually think about Universal Love and redirect your thoughts to be in confluence here. Once you bring in this vibration through your connection to how these words make you feel, you can then release this energy back into the world. Know this Love will shift all who come into contact with its vibrational frequency as it moves out into the world of form.

Will you be receptive to experience Universal Love and the gift it imparts? Embrace its beneficial, healing elements, which are not often cognitively utilized or put into play in this way. Universal Love can enter into your life when you acknowledge and accept its ever-changing potential as you enter into its expansive portal. It is then that this

Love can fully engulf your world. Do you see how it is as a result of your actions that such a gift can be drawn into the physical realm?

This is how Universal Love can be made more tangible in this reality. It is in the physicality of you connecting with the meaning given when you express this intent in your daily living. Its vibratory abundance can be drawn and released into your world. Not just reciting this one-syllable word, but feeling it and the Loving abundance it seeks to magnify accordingly. This component will enhance all it encounters. Engage with Love and seek to allow its expansiveness to move and flow as it might, to heal and restore all within its path.

Chapter 14

When in the Flow

Having absorbed the content of earlier chapters, now consider the realm of limitless potential. As you move into alignment with Universal flow, remove energetic hiccups stored in your body before you see them engage in a negative way to restrict your further progress. Seek to align yourself in the space of your intentions. If certain energetic issues have already set in, might we work together to advance change?

If you have an existing medical concern, one that has caused you to move away from your path of intention to repair your body first, what might be done? Your number one priority is for your body to heal. This has caused you to search for healing solutions so you might restore certain misaligned areas. You seek to become whole once again as you search for new insights. Renewal is sought before proceeding onto anything else.

How do you determine what is wrong? You make appointments, seek doctors' opinions, and enlist medical recommendations to know the best and most practical means to remedy what has slowed and redirected your steps.

Does any of this get to the cause and core of your issue? As we discussed earlier, oftentimes, these are topical remedies rather than long-term solutions. Can you do work concurrent to these visits, so you no longer create and recreate certain issues within your body? Can you see by releasing emotions that lie hidden in their unexpressed state, you eliminate the possibility of certain diseases manifesting in your future? These issues would take you on a detour and delay your progress in the creation of all you seek to accomplish. So if you can eliminate many of these sidesteps, you can go about doing those things that bring you joy and allow positive outcomes to take place.

And might you now look at your condition differently? Can you engage with illness from the vantage of hope and love? To no longer fight the disease, but to look at it as a suggestion for change or course correction. Now value can be attributed to all that has been given. You see, you have become aware of what you did not recognize before and can embrace each new awareness in another way. You can do so from a more enlightened, and by this, we mean aligned and loving perspective. See positive change result when you express gratitude and appreciation. When you can see value in each thing that has come to you, different steps can be enacted.

Then when you return to the doctor's office to hear test results or to receive a status report, you hear more encouraging news, having done some inner work while you waited. You held better thoughts all the while. You remained in a better mental space than earlier. You felt optimism and hope throughout that time and welcomed a chance to see if the medical reports would confirm what you most certainly already knew. When thoughts no longer constrict or restrict access, new pathways offer entrance to other portals of potential.

Are there other means or methods to determine when you are out of alignment with Universal flow? So what happens when you find yourself outside of it? Now you must add all sorts of health initiatives to your schedule as you are sidelined for a time. Your route has taken unexpected detours and delays as you must find a cure for these things and recover so you might get about your business.

Sometimes in slowing down, you uncover new insights and vistas that would have been missed without the detour. And then this health issue becomes a more vibrant occurrence as you see it and life … differently. And you recognize a value in slowing down. You take more time to study your course of direction and where you are within the journey. In the process, discoveries reveal how close you have come to certain landmarks and those intersecting roads, which would also get you closer to your desired destination.

Medical detours can sometimes reconnect you with loved ones and to valued things which were within reach all along. You just didn't make the time or fully appreciate them within your busy schedule. When you slow down a bit, you can see the many beneficial components of your life. Otherwise, you might continue to take them for granted. In your daily dealings, do you make time for those who love, need, desire, and perhaps even crave your attention?

So when a detour occurs, and you are sidelined with a disease or illness, everything else must wait. Health initiatives become your number one priority. In this scenario, repair and restoration are very important. This is only temporary, though, as you seek to re-engage in the race of life. We call it this for surely you see how you race here and there in the quest to do so many things. And will they all get done? Is it really so important, in the scheme of things, for each of them to become accomplished? Now you must stop and reconnect with life in a different manner than before to get back into its flow. To resonate with life in a way that will surely propel you more quickly back into a more desired direction.

So as illness and disease are considered, know their purpose is to allow for you to refocus and reconnect (you) to what has remained stored and unexpressed. In the lapse of time since its creation, this misaligned energy has had a metamorphosis of sorts. It has grown in magnitude and scope to become something other than what you might prefer. Now seek to connect to this disjointed, incongruent energy as it is held within. Connect, feel and then release what awaits your focus. Yet, can this energy completely dissipate if it has already transitioned into something else like a disease? Well, it depends on what you believe. If you believe all things are possible, then, of course, *this can be so.*

And so, is there a better way to recognize the need to stop and redirect your attention without disease? What other methods might be employed to cause and necessitate a pause within your day? A needed pause to reflect upon your life and why it is as it is. If these self-reflections could occur routinely, how would your life benefit and change in its current trajectory? Utilize some of the ideas and recommendations shown within these pages to enlist a fast and effective manner to clean house. Do some necessary house cleaning now. When you keep things in check, then as you age, you can do so with less pain, discomfort, and disease. Remember that age is only a number and a mental projection. Age is what you think it will be. It's a mental image you create for your future.

Try out these and other methods to alleviate unwanted drama from your life. Release any aspect you may hold to maintain a victim-status and engage in this work from a less impassioned posture. Can you do this? And then make it a point to feel those things you've created. And certainly, wouldn't you prefer to bypass all of this in the first place, if possible? This could occur when you introduce new habits, mindsets, and methodologies into your daily routine.

What might make you more mindful to readily recognize the onset of disease and to see each small pain differently? Can you address this from a different perspective and even seek to avoid some adversarial components along the way? Not to engage the mind in the what ifs of life, but to seek resolution as you know some clearing out is in order. Wouldn't that be better since detours are not readily preferred? Might you use this book as your *go-to guide*? Utilize these ideas to have a less encumbered life. In this way, you will get and remain in the flow more quickly, and thus arrive where you want to be in a more expedient way.

As you sit in reflection to release an energetic construct, also ask to remove any associated energy (within the same vibrational mix) you don't readily recall having created. The body and subconscious are great repositories for storing like-kind vibrational energy. As you work to facilitate their collective release, add language to capture other aspects that might reside there too. Ask to release all of this at once … all stored energy of your creation. If you were to individually connect to each and every emotion you have suppressed, it might take longer than you might prefer.

Know your time here on Earth is meant to be fun. Can you see by focusing on the negative what ifs of life, you more surely draw unwanted things in? Why create unexpected and unnecessary drama by doing so? When searching out solutions to the negative possibilities that might occur in your future, you draw these things to you like a magnet with your unwavering thoughts. Save your intense focus for what you desire and want. Do you see how continued mental concentration on such things draws them into your physical reality? So know your mind is a significant creator and a stronger mental magnet than you might believe.

Energy Immersion

So now we are at the point where we look to introduce a bit of magic into your life. In looking to those things that await a shift, sometimes you just need to try something a bit different that isn't the norm.

Haven't you ever stepped out to try something new to see how it felt or how something worked? Well, this is where we are today.

ELEVATE THE FREQUENCY OF ATOMS, CELLS, AND THOSE COMPONENTS THAT ARE MOVING OUT OF SEQUENCE WITH THEIR SURROUNDINGS

So here we are at the point when we might consider moving a bit differently. To move in a different step than to continue on as before. Aren't continued measures pointless when they do not bring you to where you want to be? Do you agree? So we look now to address the stepping up of frequencies that can be elevated to return energy to its original, operational mode — to bring it back to par with all in its surroundings. Do you see how this might be beneficial? So we tell you and repeat again, that all is comprised of energy. All is energy in flow.

Would you like to implement some simple steps that will produce radical changes within your body? That is what we seek to do today, to make this day unlike any other. Please do not skip the first part of this book and begin reading here, as we encourage your full understanding and your implementation of the earlier steps introduced. Some do not feel they have the time and would prefer to skip some of the outlined steps. For those we would say, might you look at your priorities. This is the most important work you can do to help your manifestations grow abundance and to have a happier and healthier you. It is also the most significant and beneficial work you can do to improve your life situation and overall health. We encourage for you to seek greater knowledge of your body and some of its underlying elements.

You are assembled with things like atoms, cells, electrons. This is where the visualization we described earlier will come into play in a significant way.

See now golden light streaming down from above to encircle you like rain. Allow this rain to fall and fill your form. Visualize your body as a transparent vessel. It is the vessel and receptacle for this Light Energy. It fills to fully saturate your physical form, and in so doing, it elevates the vibrational flow that operated there before.

YOU SEE, ALL VIBRATES DIFFERENTLY NOW

AND IN THAT DIFFERENCE,
YOU KNOW HEALING IS TAKING PLACE

See this golden light fully fill your physical form. Connect with the feeling created as you see this effervescent light radiate as it resonates accordingly within. Hear the infusion as you might listen to rain fall into the thirsty ground as it quickly absorbs this nourishing and restorative infusion. See and feel these steps as you remain focused upon this Loving energy immersion. You act as a receptacle for Universal Love to fully fill and engulf you. Sit and marinade in this energy.

In the process of all of the happenings in your life, you acquired some additional components that do not readily correspond with anything you might prefer. Will you now see any darkened or misaligned energy nestled within (you) as you set the intention for their release? Can you see each energy bubble up to the surface of your form as you seek its dissipation?

Atoms, cells, electrons are all components within the mix of your being. As such, some of these move in unison and work in alignment with the flow of your body. While other components, such as suppressed energy, were added based on decisions made when you chose previously not to connect with their associated feelings. Yes, you were born to create and feel. You were meant to fully embrace each and every creation. Yet it seems through a lack of acceptance, you preferred to push some experiences, and their associated emotions, away. By not allowing them entrance into your world, they did not surface and thus could not be fully recognized or felt.

But you see, you did create the circumstances that have determined your present moment, that which was spawned from your own energy. One could say you willed all around you into existence. And so it makes no sense that you would not want to experience what you have manifested. Again, we speak on stored energy, available for quick-release from an area in the body that aligned with its frequency. It has been drawn to the most compatible vibrational areas in your body. Those that were, and may continue to be, a vibrational match. Over time, you may discover other similar (vibrational) energy located there too.

But the principal thing is to recognize this energy can be readily accessed and released when you are ready to satisfy why it was created when you seek to feel your creation. You are its creator. And when you are ready to feel what you have created, rather than keeping this energy stored, you complete the circle, so to speak, when you choose to finish what you have begun. Universe cannot make decisions for you. You must decide by choosing what you want to do or not. So, too, recognize how your focus and intense thinking move ideas into manifestation.

VISUALIZE THIS ENERGY AS YOU SEEK TO MOVE AND THEN REMOVE WHAT YOU SEEK TO RELEASE

If there were a greater understanding of how your thoughts create from your focused attention, there might not be so much confusion on the subject. Surely, as these understandings gain a foothold, there will be a trend away from creating those things you do not want. You can see there has been much progress made on this point to date, and so all is moving in the right direction. It is when you discover and understand the significance of your thoughts and your attuned focus that true progress can be made.

And so if you think of your body as its own universe within a universe, know that disruptive energy changed various aspects within the systematic ebb and flow which once existed there. Sometimes these changes result in an abrupt shift to the way things had operated before. Initially, you see no immediate difference to your body, or the change you note does not seem significant to you. You may feel off one moment and may not give the odd feeling another thought. You rest and feel much better within hours or the next day.

Might we consider this differently? In earlier times, your world was described as a microcosm to that Greater Aspect. We tell you there are many such microcosms as worlds within worlds reside within your form. We suggest that eating styles and the like would surely change with a greater understanding of all you are fueling. How would different eating choices be employed were you to believe that other microscopic life depended upon what was ingested?

There are rotations that occur, and quite simply, misaligned or diseased cells do not spin as other cells do within a system. This is your universe or world, and so it is always important to treat it with love and respect. Not simply because it is your body, but because it is so much more. Every aspect of you is living and alive with momentum and purpose. Each component does have purpose. So when you introduce ingredients that take it away from its routine flow, well, that is noteworthy. So again, consider how your body maintains itself each moment of the day without your direct oversight. This is truly an awe-inspiring thing.

So as you introduce a new vibration into the dynamics of your body and that energy becomes stored, its vibration will continue to resonate there. It does, in a manner, intensify, for it is working against what has been naturally occurring there before. As it continues to vibrate, it enlists and draws more like-kind energy to itself and thus can grow in measure. You do, in time, feel a change. Whether or not you recognize this or just try to continue on, well, it will need to be dealt with at some point. Suppression can only mask what you seek to push down for a while. But in time, it will surface. Its purpose is to be felt and recognized as one of your many creations.

If an injury or illness redirects your steps by putting you back on track, might you see it as a blessing? Ideally, would it be possible to bless and be grateful for each occurrence? They are, in many ways, trail markers and provide signs to make sure you are on the right path. When you bless, rather than fight anything, any occurrence, you engage with a higher frequency. This frequency works to elevate and raise the vibration when it is out of sequence with neighboring cells. Healthy cells do not resonate with the same vibrational frequency as those whose pattern is jarred and disjointed. Such behavior seems to work against those that flow in harmony to one another. Some might say this is a symbiotic relationship that is not beneficial to its primary host.

Are you receptive to the belief that you can create positive change within your body when you introduce new measures to try out in your life? Without this mental agreement, there can be little advancement beyond this point.

CAN YOU BELIEVE IT IS POSSIBLE TO ACCOMPLISH EVERYTHING YOU DESIRE

This is the first understanding you must concur with to progress effectively beyond this page. Know to the core of your being how you do truly control your own destiny. With that understanding, you champion your life and all aspects that occur there. You see, when your life focuses on only one version of reality, it is time for a shakeup and for you to *wake up*.

Some individuals have nothing much going on except for their next doctor's appointment or their next medical procedure, and this is not living. This is merely existing and seeing how you might engage the mind to create yet another medical occurrence for you to engage in. Or to continue to reignite what should already be in your rearview mirror.

Do you see there are other options you can create for this life? And in that life, you can manifest a different future for your later years. Retirement is man-made, and so as you acquiesce to its parameters, know you need not do so. And if you fall into the uncertainties and what ifs created in the space of not knowing your future, what then? If you stop engaging your mind with appropriate stimulation, then you might think slowing down and getting old is what you are meant to do and be.

We say this is not so. We look to those with experience to give understanding and guidance to the youth of the world. Let them know you are relevant so you might earn their trust and respect. Show them you know what you are talking about here. So look to give back if you are not currently doing so. Get out of your homes and off of your couches to engage and energize others. This will give you added purpose in your golden years. Yes, they are known to be golden for a reason. You have accumulated understandings and knowledge that can be shared and imparted to those of a lesser experience.

Energy Orbs

Changing focus, might we ask about energy orbs? Have you played with them before? Might we play a bit now? Sit in a meditative posture, palms of your hands facing up on your lap. We want you to focus for a time on your hands and to feel the energy that pulsates and expands in them.

Feel and grow this energy now. Allow for this energy to move up your hands and course through your body, although the intensity of focus is to remain in your hands. Can you feel its tingling, energetic flow? Continue to focus on this pulsating energy as your focus heightens the experience. Focus to feel this energy specifically in your fingertips as they remain cupped in your lap. See and feel this sensation for a few minutes.

Visualize ever-growing, fire-like orbs of energy. See them intensify and spark. See them jump about as you cradle them in the palms of each hand. Intently focus upon the golden energy which pulsates there. See these orbs rapidly flicker and spark as they emit iridescent, pulsating bursts of energy as you continue to cradle them in your hands. See them sparkle as they dance about. Now slowly draw your hands up, so they are raised and parallel in front of you. Continue your focus on the orbs as you watch their two forms begin to coalesce and merge ... one to the other.

As their sparks fly about, see their other components glow and sparkle. Recognize these orbs do not simply burn as would a physical flame, nor or they likened to a physical flame. They have an iridescent radiance emanating from them. These are energetic orbs which ignite to fill vacuums and voids. Visualize to see these energy orbs pulsate as they move in a figure-eight formational flow. Watch them mix and mingle as they dance with purpose and symmetry. Seek for these two golden orbs to merge together during this process. In their union, they intensify. Its pulsating glow is likened to the brilliance of an energetic illuminated light.

Seek to grow this singular orb dimensionally as it pulses between your hands. Stretch your hands out to expand its size, or conversely, move your hands closer together to compress its form. Now add heat to the mix. Feel an amplified (yet comforting) heat pulsating from its formation. This orb radiates an energy of renewal. See and feel this glowing, bright white energy. Compress and expand its spatial form. Now lightly contract and expand this orb between the expanse of your hands. Feel this newly created energy as you play in the wonderment of it. Grow this energy orb by stopping every inch or so to create the preferred dimensions as you see and feel this Light Energy.

VISUALIZE, EXPERIENCE, FEEL

CONSCIOUSLY ENGAGE

When feeling is added to the mix, you generate a component that is energetically aligned to its creator's focus. Do you seek to infuse your form to fill a void or vacuum? Might you move to set the intention that this orb is to infuse new energy into an area that is currently out of sequence or less than you desire? Might you qualify all to Source as you seek such measures? Seek a restorative infusion. In this way, your body can integrate it and utilize this energetic infusion to assist in the body's full recovery and originating functionality, health, and vitality.

Complete the steps given above. Now move this energy into that preferred area by placing your hands over the location where integration is sought. See this energy becoming absorbed as the absorption aspect is engaged. Intend for this to occur. Qualify all. Might you now play in this way?

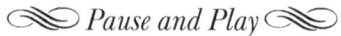

Pause and Play

As you do this work, develop, distinguish and feel this energy. Connect to it and recognize it is manifested energy of your intention. Place it where you perceive it to be most beneficial. Direct this energy into that defined area where you want its effects localized to manifest wholeness. If you do not know specifically, might you ask?

As you place energy into one area, visualize healthy and whole cells engaging with this newly formed energy as it flows to fill vacuums and voids created by the release work you have done or as you do it. As your hands direct its course, let them linger over that area to allow for this energy to become energetically absorbed. During this time, it is important to stay focused and mentally attached, but not to place words into your mind during this part of the process. Know you are releasing newly created energy into an area and are simply a conduit for its transfer. Can you feel it becoming absorbed? Can you feel the energy going into those areas where it is best used by your body?

Know your body understands what has been added to it. It will seek to integrate the energy you've provided. It will acknowledge its presence as it integrates with it. It is your acceptance and belief that will make this so. So look very closely. Can you visualize the atoms and other cellular components that make up your body? Access a photo of healthy atoms as you focus inwardly now.

Focus and feel the added mobility this energy provides. Can you sit and now add thought-forms when you visualize cell recalibration? Be selective and discerning with what you view. Look only upon those things that are whole and healthy as you focus now. See this pure, newly created energy deep within your body where you would like it to be infused. Focus on this for a few minutes, then release the thought-form. Ask mentally for this energy to be integrated and to become synergistic with your being.

See everything in rhythmic flow as your body engages with it. If there is anything that is vibrationally less than what you have introduced, ask for its alignment and recalibration. You seek now for the flow to return to its original state as you see only whole and healthy cells there. Ask for anything of a lesser vibration which has been disrupted or interrupted to release, recalibrate and re-engage. Ask for your energy to be reset as you focus upon this now.

Recognize within this process, as throughout your life, you will be directly in charge of the thoughts you keep. When holding certain thoughts, you will be able to restore and allow your body to reformat cells as you work to release what no longer serves you. You can easily do this with a bit of practice and will soon find you can shift into this mode with ease. It is only a matter of time before you are able to enlist other components that will build upon this practice. This is the first step you might undertake. These first steps will need to flow comfortably from you in order for the next step to be introduced. Seek to further such integration as you incorporate these things into the field of limitless potential.

⁓ Turn the page from limitation to liberation ⁓

Reset the Subconscious

You must determine what you want from this life and when it is time to turn the page. We offer these initial remedies as a means for you to play in the field of unlimited possibility. Continue with insights and the medical advice of your doctors, along with their tests and procedures, but work also in the manner described. You might find when the next tests are taken, less disease is found than before, or that nothing remains. See only the best outcome. We advise your focus to be on your continued progress and for your mental course of action to remain in a positive realm. When you focus on those negative what ifs, the mind has a way of playing them continually within its loop of thinking. We want to stop the loop and disengage it from running in the background of your mind. So let us focus on some other considerations now.

DIRECT THE SUBCONSCIOUS TO DELETE OLD PATTERNS AND DO A RESET

Ask your subconscious to store all which has been given and to delete those which are not of service to you now. Sit with this request.

Do you see how your body and mind will take direction from you when you lead accordingly? Can you compare these actions to how you might work with a computer to restore it to its original settings? If you don't, might you consider this with one exception? Reset the subconscious to the pristine version held by Universe for it will include the information we have imparted here. Reset, as Universe might suggest, to those settings which are for your highest and best use.

So take the lead and continue with this work for a time. If you do not know when to move forward or when it would be best to move onto the next step, ask to be given direction. Remember to ask also those questions you want answered before retiring each night. Look to receive insights as you awaken. There are times when you shift between sleep and an awakened state. It is the time between these two modes where you might find your many insights and where your answers lie. Record what is given so such insights are not lost.

Dreams might also be recorded. The key here is to determine what the symbology means to you. Each dream is specific to the individual, and so if you rely on another to interpret them, you will have the mix of their instruction rather than your own. Always seek to receive inner counsel as you plot your next course of action.

Certainly elicit input, recommendations and consider all options, but, ultimately, do seek counsel within. You have all the necessary components to make each determination. When you ask another individual to make your decisions, you are yielding control of the circumstances to their level of understanding. They can never know all the components as you know them.

Also, ask in prayer. Whomever you know as your Higher Source should be enlisted, as well as your Unseen Entourage. There are many who await your call. And know your call will always produce an answer. This has and will continue to be so. Ask to be directed toward what you seek or for a teacher to step in. A teacher will always appear to provide you with the necessary insights and instruction when you are amenable to take your next step.

We support you and your endeavors, and so know, we too, are available to address your questions and concerns as you move about seeking more in this life. Simply ask ... when you are ready.

As no two Souls are looking for the exact same accessories or costume as they move about in this life, so know, individuality is just that. You are unique. You cannot be compared to or associated with another because of distinct attributes no one else has but you. When one points out a similarity, do you like their comparison or being compared in this way? Do you see the commonality, or do you see something else? Is it a feature or a trait? Your uniqueness is for a purpose, and we will say it is fun to sometimes hear how another thinks but do not focus on their assessments of you. Seek to keep your thoughts from becoming influenced by their opinions, which exist from a limited perspective. Their rose-colored glasses and perceptions of you are inconsequential within your life's dynamic. This is the mirroring aspect we discussed earlier, as their words are for their benefit, not yours.

So in contemplating your health and healing, what more can be given? We seek your expansion, rather than being sidelined by a disease or illness. So much is in the formulation and acceptance of your mind. The mind often focuses on the worst-case scenario and accepts pronouncements made. Although it strives to do so, the mind knows it cannot control each and every situation.

Perhaps consider this. Do you acknowledge a cold when you experience a runny nose initially? Or when a medical test is run, do you readily settle into what the doctor tells you when they announce some abnormality seen as they seek to understand and diagnose the situation? What energy do you place upon their words, and moreover, what do you silently think? Do you start justifying the illness as it is placed upon your doorstep? Do you rationalize why it is here when you don't even know for sure if what they have interpreted is accurate? Rather, is it possible to not accept, to not justify, and to remain centered for a time? As you consider what's been said, do some immediate work before your next doctor's visit. In this way, you can begin to shift things within you. Do this work concurrent to theirs, even as you seek a second and third opinion in the process.

We do advise for you to stay centered and to remain in a questioning mode throughout this time, but to not necessarily accept what you have heard from this one analysis or diagnosis. To remain in a degree of wonderment keeps the mind in check a bit. You have heard only one interpretation, and really they won't know this or that for certain until all the tests are run. They need to run a series of tests or at least another test or two. So perhaps don't judge the situation with such a critical eye or ask for worst-case scenarios. Only ask these health or medical professionals to share the best outcome. Discuss better scenarios initially. The mind tries to outwit you to introduce drama during the interim. Well, that is pure folly.

So know as you are ready to read more of what might be, let us say that we welcome your interest and desire to heal. In this vein, will you consider other options available to you now? Do you find you have exhausted existing remedies, or is it that you seek more? When you think on your molecular structure and the atoms and cells within your system, do you wonder if a vibration could be introduced that would allow for the rotation of the unhealthy cells to be recalibrated? We have discussed this, but wonder if you would again consider the vibrational nature of the cell and that it does vibrate. When infected with this or that disease, it takes on another nature. One that doesn't resonate with surrounding cells.

In this understanding, it resists working in a compatible way with other cells and so it moves away from a more concentric flow. Let us say that it begins to work in an inharmonious manner. In the new relationship which exists with the cells it might have previously worked with in unity, it resonates differently. So a new dynamic has been established ... one that doesn't flow as before and one that offers countermeasures to maintain an inharmonious structure in relation to other cells. This energy has an independent, incongruent nature and one that doesn't readily seek to work in conjunction with, but rather, in opposition to those operating there before.

For example, cancer is a most insidious disease and one that seemingly manifests often. There are many who seek the final discovery to cure this condition as they combat or fight it. Do you see how its vibration works against those who undertake such a discovery? However, you might look at cancer and work with it to see a value instead of emitting a dread of sorts that causes other things to spring forth and develop.

In seeing the benefit and giving gratitude for what it portends, would you consider to work with it instead of in opposition to it? Perhaps to be grateful that it has been diagnosed so measures can be taken to alleviate it. As work progresses from the aspect of gratitude, do you see how a positive vibrational component will allow for the shifting of these cells to occur in a good way? Seek to engage from a positive stance, rather than to engage in a fight against this or any disease.

Work in resonance with the disease, rather than in opposition to its survival. Do not fight it or anything. It is in the fighting that a disconnection occurs. Disease is used as an indicator of what is not preferred; it's unwanted and often feared. This situation is further compounded when a variety of negative scenarios run repetitively through the mind. Can you see how this does not serve any benefit unless positive rather than negative points are pondered instead?

So what is the best course of action, especially if there are cancer cells involved? Do you believe it is possible to change the vibration of a cancer cell? Can these be shifted to vibrationally be in step with those cells which are healthy? In other words, since collectively they resonate differently, can they shift to mirror healthier cells in their proximity? Is that possible? We say this can be so. What will enable more promising outcomes to appear? How might you change the vibration of something you cannot see? Perhaps you are unsure your work will allow for the change you seek. You will not know for sure until another test is run to see what effect your efforts have had on this disease.

We tell you this can be so with cancer and also with any other disease. You can shift the vibration from the current one to step up the next, so there is a degree of improvement that can be quantitatively measured. It begins with what you believe you can do and accomplish here. Can you have a firm conviction or an unwavering belief for this possibility to become real? So choose with whom you share this undertaking, for it is something you must stay fixed upon to reap the positive outcome you seek. You want to reinforce personal beliefs (when possible) with those who share your hopes and dreams. Do so selectively. Choose to enlist support wisely.

Also, might you reframe and refrain from considering the cancer, per se? There is a strong vibratory pattern, or morphic field, associated with this disease, and it has cultivated what we might term a vibration of fear. And so, disengage with this terminology and seek to call it by another name … a name that has no dreaded association to anything in particular. Perhaps even consider a name of endearment or something fun. In any regard, it will shift how you think of it and how others think about it and you, if you will engage with it from a more playful vantage.

And so, where does the gathering and knowing of so many initial steps lead us as we pivot from this point to the next? You have come from a Light Body or Essence of Being, and when you leave this earthly domain, that is where you will return. As such, you came from complete perfection. You moved into a denser form to experience life, the emotions, and the ebb and flow of existence here. Thus, perfection is not to be achieved on this planet.

First, it is unnecessary to spend a great degree of time to elicit perfection. It is not the reason you are here. If it were, you would not be on this physical, emotionally felt planet. You would be in another dimension. So let go of any need to be perfect or to feel that perfection is necessary as this does not serve a purpose in your day-to-day dealings. It is understandable to want to bring forward what is the best thing, vibrationally speaking, that you can enact. Do you understand the difference we seek to impart here?

The densities felt on this planet are not fully appreciated or remembered when preparing for another incarnation. Thus when a lifestream enters this physical dimension, the emotions or expressions sought appear magnified and greater than anticipated. What is meant by this is the density here allows for a deeper, more fully felt reality. This is why so many Souls chose to come here. Each came to feel the experience they sought to understand more completely. They wanted to fully feel.

So as we move forward in a new direction, one that allows your body as your temple to exist in a fuller capacity let us move in keeping to be more in alignment with your original blueprint or life plan. Keep an open mind, as some of these words and practices will be new to you … although they are not truly new.

And so, we look to reintroduce what has been about you all along. To access more tools to garner and engage. We welcome your thoughts, comments, and questions. It is in the engagement of these methods that will allow for your restoration, and so it would be most beneficial for you to enlist and embrace them. Don't merely read words without experiencing their practices, or place this book back on your shelf to try again another day. Although you do assimilate what you read at many levels, action is also necessary, for you will not reap benefits as by mere osmosis.

Entering In

As you enter into doing this work, is it really work or something wanted and yearned for? Isn't it a joy when you are able to connect to something that allows you a new perspective and another way to engage with life? Let's focus your mind in a new way that will keep it disengaged from disbelief or other folly.

Might you enter into your meditations, if you have not done so before, from a feeling of holiness and gratitude? Understanding from this vantage the level of mastery you desire to draw forth. Thus, when you enter from this preferred state, you enlist wonder and awe into the mix. You then set about to consciously engage from a different vibratory level.

In the un-knowing-ness that exists at this level, you surrender to something Greater than you are in this physical form. Yes, this is your posture when in recognition and in the realization that Universal Source has a greater awareness than can be known from the more limited vantage from which you now reside. Universe knows the bigger, more expansive picture as your view is currently filtered through the mind. The mind has constructs that do not allow for the full realization to be understood through its limited scope or premise.

As you enter now into this space, incorporate some additional practices that will allow for a holiness to be felt. If it is to light a candle, burn incense, or to do some other preferred practice, might you take these steps to start your engagement? The intention is to out-picture a devotion for these works in accordance with your own personal beliefs. This practice should be symbolic of your feelings and intent; it also shows a degree of appreciation for what you are certain to receive back from these experiences as they will surely enhance your life as they return full circle back to you.

Consider playing uplifting music softly in the background to also enhance each meditational experience. Play only what will intensify and not distract from this endeavor. There are musical frequencies which have been in existence previously that are being released again in this time through attuned artists and composers. These musical creations will align and elevate your being with their inspired melodies. Alignment occurs when you relinquish your foothold to a previously held vibrational energy allowing another flow to re-establish itself. It is your openness to do so, through the surrender component, that more can be given.

When you meditate, put into play these new understandings. Listen to musical compositions that enable you to effortlessly align and leave you resonating appropriately. Might you feel a degree of contentedness? Allow their notes to be those that raise your mood. Choose a vibration that is inspiring — or might we say inspirational? Engage this thought process when you select your background music. As you sit in a comfortable position, choose one that doesn't encourage sleep to result or one that might constrict your energy flow. Your preferred posture will allow energy to easily and effortlessly course through your body. Find what works best for you. Here we move into a meditation.

Now focus on your breath as you breathe in and out, slowly and intently. Breathe deeply to engage the diaphragm. See your breath traveling throughout your body. See it move down to your feet, coursing throughout your form. Breathe deeply while you remain focused on your breath. Become aware of your toes and fingers as you feel them tingle. Now send Love, Universal Love to all body parts. Take some time to do this now — focus and feel.

Visualize and see Light Energy as it flows throughout your body. Set the intention that it is to touch each and every cell, atom, electron that fills your form. See it as white light, flecked with gold, or perhaps as a golden-white light. See the color your body aligns with and focus on that energy now. Visualize it entering at the base of your neck, through the crown of your head, or at another preferred location. As it enters, feel its pulsations. Watch it flow throughout your body, down one side and then up the other in a wave of vibrant energy. See this pulsating Light Energy surge throughout your body, filling you fully and completely. Engage this process a number of times before stopping. Again focus and feel.

Can you feel the resonance which remains? Do you feel this Light Energy as it continues to pulsate and resonate within? If you do not feel a slight tingling, see if you have crossed your legs or are sitting in a posture that might somewhat restrict and constrict that which will surely resonate after having touched all. In this way, it leaves its fingerprint behind as its resonance marks all it touches. Align, focus and feel this energy now.

THESE ASPECTS BRING YOU TO A STATE
OF EXPECTANCY AND LOVE

Be grounded as you do this and other works. Grounded as you remain present in this most wondrous moment in time. Anchor yourself now if you have not already done so. In this way, you might move more readily to connect within and with Source Energy. Align yourself in the connectivity you seek.

Sit in a posture that is again aligned to bring you to an enlightened state of being. Visualize energy coming from above, flowing in and through you. This energy enters your head as it courses through your body, proceeding into the ground beneath your feet. As this energy continues onward to the Earth's center, see it branch out as roots are to a tree. Continue as you visualize this energy surge forth to further stabilize you in becoming anchored and grounded with the day.

As you clear the mind of other distractions, watch this vibratory Light Energy flow through your body. See it touch each aspect in need of healing and visualize each component return to the wholeness of its original design.

Feel your energy flowing and growing. Stay with the feeling emanating from within. See a fiery light expand in dimension and scope as it courses through your body. Watch the fiery spark within grow in unlimited intensity. This is what you might sit with for a few minutes.

Do this work in conjunction with continued focus on your breath as you breathe deeply now. Breathe deeply and hold the breath — briefly. Repeat and hold to a longer count. Expand and grow this practice. By re-engaging Flame Ignite again and often, you establish and anchor that which is of significance. Integrate and infuse Flame Ignite in this way.

Flame Ignite

L ife for me is very precious.
It is a reflection of my inner me.
As I see life and all its wonders,
let me bask in that which sets me free.
Free from pain and consequence;
free from energetic woes.
Free from doubt and consternation;
free from all that I do now let go.

I AM open to forgiveness, not from others, but from self.
I do now see how this holds the key to unlock my full,
expansive potentiality.

Bring that Aspect that lies hidden,
dormant less expansive now,
to engage and resurrect It
as It moves throughout me now.
There is but a small Flame burning;
It is yet a mere glow.
Let me elevate Its yearning, as I invoke It,
It does now grow.

Consume all that feels downtrodden,
less than the full potential I AM to Be.
I know my life will be more centered
to flow in grace synergistically.

Flame Ignite
(continued)

I release doubt, remorse, fear as I let my story out.
It is there, amongst the Flame
    which now begins to dance about.
Let me stoke this glowing Ember
    as It strengthens with delight.
It is a light so bright and bold,
    I AM so grateful to behold the Love It does ignite.

Always present, yet now so bright.
It has waited to fully ignite
    Its beautiful flame of colors bright
    that now do quiver and quake with delight.
See the flutter, do you see It growing exponentially?
It is no longer my hidden treasure,
    for now to It I do lay claim.
I realize that God Source resides within
    as I watch the momentum, it begins.

Yes, this Flame resides within me for sure
    as It expands this day and burns ever pure.
For as I acknowledge my connection to Source,
    Universal Love floods in and through to thus reinforce
    as Love and Light do merge to Ignite,
    transmute and go forth.

Flame Ignite
(continued)

To enable this flow, I know this to be true to my core
    and believe as never before.
In this knowing, I will resolve to restore
    all that's amiss and so much more.

I acknowledge, Love and do nurture this Flame.
In this connection to God Source I do now remain.
It does emblazon me within,
    as I feel Its Light and Its Love
    which empowers my being
    to strengthen my life force from below to above.

In knowing and being,
    I do reinforce and recognize that in due course,
    all will lessen,
    dissolve and no longer burden my life force.

Flaming, pulsating, the Fire that did shimmer
    now burns and expands to run like a river.
The flow does move to heal and restore
    as It strengthens my foundation down to my core.

I feel this, know and believe Love is key.
As all Aligns within to now set me free.

Now settle into the space from which you reside. If you do not feel you move in concurrence with this flow, then continue in the repetition of these words. You should gain a resonance and begin to feel the vibrational mix within you. It is best to sample each thing to see what resonates with you. It is a subjective decision and based on the frequency you individually evoke.

Set an intention to engage healing. Recognize and see this healing in your mind's eye as if each healing had already occurred. Feel as if you were already whole and healed. The body will begin to respond to your commands and direction when you mask the pain for a time and work through an issue with a centeredness of purpose. When you hold a belief on any topic, more is drawn to you. So in this case, you are already beginning to heal as you draw these properties in.

Find gratitude in each experience. With a bit of humor, you can lighten any load and fully ignite the healing process to begin anew. As you settle into the space of doing this work, realize that you have access to a series of gifts which we reference as your internal tools. These aspects bring you to a state of expectancy and Love.

Do you have expectations of what specific tools await your discovery? You see, these tools were crafted having resulted from your past energetic accomplishments. Since they are of your creation, they remain with you for use upon your focused attention. They become activated by your desire to reconnect with them once again in this day.

As you sit in meditation and stillness, look internally for the answers you seek, as all waits within. Life awaits your energetic engagement to enlist, dislodge and implement tools to be used this day. As you sit in contemplation or meditation, clear your mind from focus on daily activities or checklists which await completion. Instead, allow insights to enter into a blank mental canvas after having cleared out unnecessary banter to create a welcoming space. Otherwise, as thoughts race about during the day, you will become distracted and miss those things that await your discovery. Be receptive and invite insights to enter in. How else will you get the answers you seek unless you create an inviting mental space in anticipation of all which will be provided. Become clear of the clutter.

You are an amazing and marvelous repository of many things. Seek to access the tools you have developed, created, and refined in past times from previous incarnations. They are accessible through your desire to engage them into existence once again. These unique tools are nestled within and await being ignited into action. Call them into your present-day reality when you acknowledge, accept, and seek to experience your treasures. Emblazon your world in their renewal and activation. When you infuse your present reality with past energetic creations, you can speed up today's manifestations. Activate and make them available when you seek their engagement in this day.

Chapter 15

Hidden Treasures

Now let us spend some time to provide some additional information regarding those internal tools, or hidden treasures, which await connection within. We have said before that you entered this life with all you need to accomplish, experience, and be. Can you accept this truth and believe it to be so?

All lies within, and these things can be accessed when this understanding is fully embraced. Acknowledge and know this, for it is most key. In this vein, Universe also engages through your thoughts, words, and corresponding actions of support. These are those which reinforce your beliefs. As you do so, you move into an aligned oneness to express and out-picture all that awaits manifestation.

So what are those tools or gifts alluded to, and how might you know them? If you were not aware of them earlier or have forgotten about them, how might you draw upon those tools now? Do you ever feel you have more than you need in order to do those things you would like to accomplish within this life, or have you been anxiously waiting to discover more? Even though you recognize your gift is the creation of your unique vibration when you are in a manifestation mode, how can you connect with this vibration to bring it into being and make it physical?

Can you readily access all avenues available to speed up such self-discoveries? Is one method better or more efficient than another? Do you ponder such questions? Might you ask? Yes, you can most certainly speed up this quest. Yet know there is no timetable or best time to discover your hidden treasures. All will manifest in the right time for you. What do we mean by this, and what sort of treasures might await your discovery?

Many reading these words will acknowledge having had other lifetimes. Within those embodiments, you gained knowledge and certain skills. Why not ask for aspects of your collective understanding to come into your life now? Do you seek to explore this possibility? If so, ask Universe to give you access to those skills you ascertained then. You can also call into the present moment aspects of those things you have yet to learn in this lifetime. You can call them forward into this reality if you will but ask and believe.

WHAT MIGHT UNIVERSE BRING TO YOU NOW BY ASKING FOR IT TO BE

Consider this premise as you would an intention. You will want to express to Universe what you wish to access. This includes what you have already learned, future tools, and even the mantle carried by another whose skills you would like to expand upon. Ask during meditation, in a meditative state, to have insights and a greater awareness brought in. What most valued insight might propel your existence forward to help in your advancement? What might be shared? Is it simply enough to trust and believe Universe? Remember to ask and qualify all.

So as you set intentions for your future, might you phrase your request to Universe in a more expansive way to draw in what has already manifested for you and awaits a connection to you now? Might you acknowledge this portal of potential?

So often, life is seen as a very lateral experience. But what if that existence were a three-dimensional hologram with many facets you simply cannot see, in your mind's eye or outwardly, because of the mere physicality of it? If existence is truly more like a hologram than as seen by you, would you not look at things a bit differently? Could you see more out-shoots of possibility and more diverse outcomes than what you see from a one-dimensional reality? There are so many more options when you change your perspective and seek the newness a revised vantage offers. And that is our purpose. To have these words serve as a springboard when you use such a platform to shift your focus — to look at life with endless and alternate opportunities from a vast assortment of potentialities. Do you see from this vantage, life can be out-pictured in a variety of scenarios and not limited by the constructs in place because you are physically placed?

Alternate realities exist. These understandings will expand to shift how you see things. If you no longer limit yourself to this vantage or view, can you then choose another? And in that second look, might a shift in your perception occur? Consider this line of logic as we introduce new avenues for your exploration. If you no longer see things in a strictly defined way, but rather as more open-ended and limitless, then you will have evermore options to consider. Your intentions may be restricted because of the physical limitations imposed by the mind, which restricts beliefs held in the psyche. Once those limitations are removed, you will be able to move more in keeping with the intentions of your heart. One that is in alignment with the hopes and aspirations you sought to experience before you entered the portal of this life. With this one understanding, you can choose between so many more realities. And as you remove self-imposed limitations, you are open to more diverse considerations. As we continue, let us consider yet another tool.

Might you engage with the purity of your Soul? As with new-fallen snow, you can also pull into your field of awareness what is pristine and pure, for this is yours to claim. In pulling in and resonating with an aspect of your Soul's Essence, you can align in a different way than before. Not to say you will always want to reside in this magnificent energy, yet it can be most beneficial for you to feel this Spiritual Aspect when you are in need of a calming component.

As you are seated in a meditative posture, bring your Essence into focus and feel it blanketing you. Acknowledge your connection to Source Energy. Ask for that vibration to be felt within. Utilize the same steps as you used for Universal Love to blanket you. Visualize and balance any frequencies that need an adjustment. Know when you align with that Greater Part of you, a more centered state of consciousness will always result. Once engaged, you can experience, for a time, the absence of stress as you bring in greater clarity of thought. Slow your mind to allow for new solutions to appear and resolve former challenges.

Feel your Essence as it overlays and blankets your physical form. Do you feel a comfort and corresponding Love resonate in your midst? It is by your intention that you amplify this connection. Feel this as you experience both more fully.

As you know, you are much more than this physical form. You are a Spiritual Being who has taken this form to experience life, to understand emotions and the feelings they create. In this physicality, such emotions are felt in a more significant way than was remembered prior to entering this physical form. Although we have said this before, it is worth noting again. In this physical dimension, emotions are recalled differently than in the spiritual realm. There is a degree of forgetfulness that occurs. These emotions become intertwined with Earth's densities, resulting in the highs and lows that are more deeply felt here.

All the twists and turns experienced on the physical plane accelerate and intensify what is felt. If someone wants to feel compassion, how do you truly understand what compassion feels like without experiencing personal loss? You feel and appreciate love more completely when you suffer an opposing feeling. If everything were perfect, how would you ever know what you really have without its opposite? Without experiencing the contrasting component, you cannot fully appreciate its opposing aspect.

So as we proceed, know there is much more available to experience, for the mind cannot comprehend many things beyond this physical world ... beyond what it is experiencing now. So know the imagination is the best gateway to other possibilities and probabilities. All have potential existence when you allow them entrance into the Nowness of this time.

Do you see then, you can first access another realm through your imagination? When advancements are seen before their time, they appear as mumbo jumbo and nonsensical. This is especially true when conceptualized creations appear prematurely. Their significance and value may not have been fully understood in an earlier life experience. New realities are dreams that have become realized. Many cannot access a visionary's inventiveness. It is a multilayered, multi-tiered miracle of sorts when someone dares to dream outside of what is considered to be standard and conventional. When they operate outside of the norm, in many ways, they move into uncharted waters. They release the routine and embrace the unknown. They play in the field of possibility and promise. They move out of the mental box of what is known as they shift into the expansiveness of what is yet to be discovered.

Some have the vision and ability to move beyond the normal realm of understanding, while others do not. To push past boundaries means to release self-imposed limitations — imposed by those who do not dare to dream or seek the newness of another path. Followers tend to continue on a well-worn pathway, avoiding the work of clearing out a new trail. Maybe the dogma, or the controversy to step out-of-step, keeps them from forging into untested waters. These followers prefer to accept a more traditional route, missing the promise and miracle found in each new day — the promise seen by visionaries who seek a different tomorrow.

In this vein of thought, we ask you to embrace new concepts as you move forward to stretch the imagination and those limitations established by the mind. We seek your understanding as you internalize new possibilities. Without your implementation of these new avenues, they will remain as mere words on a page. But if you will seek to engage them within your life, then you will have the advantage of their limitless potential. You always have the opportunity to change the momentum if you so choose. Or to accelerate the speed of those things you wish to more rapidly accomplish.

There is a fine line of differentiation which we must acknowledge. Sometimes you must read things at a different level than you would normally. As you are aware, much instruction is given at a level for the many. As you revisit some previous teaching, do you find you are no longer where you once were spiritually, or might we say energetically?

Now as you read the same words, a different level of understanding comes into play. As time has progressed, the words have taken on a new meaning. They seem to be so much more than before. So when you return yet again, sometimes many years later, and pick up that same book and reread its pages, the passages move you to yet another understanding. You will have found an even deeper meaning through the messages that magically appear before you. They impart more than you recognized earlier.

Many times, what appears to be the central premise is masked a bit so that many can glean value from the same words. Not everyone is ready to take that next step. We tell you that each individual is where they need to be. They need exactly what they take away and internalize. If they do not yet know their next step, it is not the right time to embrace it. If it is the right time, then the instruction is internalized from a renewed perspective, and you experience life from a corresponding level of understanding to mirror back your intentions.

It is key to withhold and not elicit judgment. Such rationalizations are often enlisted to protect the one who judges from something they simply don't understand, or that doesn't make sense to them. Is this the best way to protect against the unknown, or is this ploy engaged when there is a need to feel above the circumstance or another? Whether you need protection or are disavowing something unproven, seek open-mindedness. If you self-limit through your thoughts, you will impede the ability to conceptualize new methodologies. As you read these pages, know your subconscious will understand these words. Return again when you want to re-engage with these concepts from another level so you might garner and implement different insights not recognized before.

So begin by acknowledging your body is not necessarily as you see it, as it is pure vibrational energy. You have known this. Shift and reshape what you want to change. When you engage your mind in this fashion, you can co-create changes in your world. Revamp the vessel that harbors your Spirit.

Surely you have heard, read, or known of someone who has changed their situation by right-thinking applications. We want to take that understanding and build upon it somewhat. So imagine a time when you have had an existing injury or disease. Perhaps you took a vaccine so you wouldn't catch the flu. Yet you caught it, or did it catch you? You were ambushed by the various symptoms that waylaid you. What if you could change that? Minimize or reduce havoc created by disease by redirecting the way the virus impacts your form? This is possible if you are open to receiving instruction and remembering to implement insights rather than merely reading or reciting words. Be present; recognize when it is time to choose those thoughts that will advance you.

So imagine that you need only to focus on something whole and pure to achieve your objective. Something that will redirect your thoughts from a woe is me mentality to something more aligned with your Lineage. So you visualize and actually look upon something beautiful within nature. You see no flaw with this thing of beauty as you set your sights upon it now. Recognize all of the minute components that have drawn you to this thing as you look upon it. Strive to connect with it as you feel its vibration resonating in sequence by an inner connection to it. Realize you are not separate from it in any way. You are, in essence, one with it as it is one with you. See its wholeness, beauty, and perfection. As you focus on this, can you envision your energy merging with it in this oneness?

If you have a blemish, is it something you can easily correct? Is it something that can be made whole to out-picture itself in a different manner? Is it something permanent or is it in some transitory phase?

Really, all within your body is in some phase of transition, but how do you see it? Is a tooth shifting, a toe moving inward such as a bunion, or something else? Focus upon something you see as a thing which can be shifted. Something moveable, not permanent, or set in stone.

Now, can you align your focus with something that represents beauty and wholeness? It could be a dead tree if you see the beauty and perfection within the shell of a tree. Even in its death, it brings life to the soil as it returns to bring nutrients in its decomposition. It teams with life in many ways. So pick the item within nature that represents and resonates perfection, beauty, and wholeness to you. It may not be this, but something else, as you consider what is beautiful and vital.

We would recommend focusing on something you can tangibly see and touch. So where have you decided to place your attention? If it is on a television image, a picture viewed on a laptop, or in a magazine, these images may not connect you in the way needed to enact this exercise. If you have access to three-dimensional imagery, this may work, but we would recommend keeping your focus on something within your immediate proximity in nature.

So when you find that vibrant item of beauty and wholeness, focus upon it. Recognize it may have an imperfection or blemish, which you discover during your intense concentration of its features, but that's okay. Continue to look and see each and every aspect. Marvel at the uniquenesses of this tree or perhaps a blooming flower, as each is distinct and one of a kind.

For the purposes of an example, we will focus upon the formation of a bunion. Ponder the idea of a tree, with its straight stature in the mind's eye, and then relate it back to the misaligned toe. Select a tree that represents the beauty and wholeness imparted by its majestic form and strength. Now seek alignment with it. Project and align this upward reaching tree upon this inward moving toe as you envision this tree overlaid upon it. Visualize all its tall branches and leaves that rustle in the wind. But also recognize this tree has been around for many years and it is not likely to bend or move from its unyielding position.

Visualize to see the tree merge to meld with the toe. See the toe from the vantage of this magnificent tree as it becomes superimposed upon the big toe. Focus also upon the upright positioning of the tree. In this way, its strength and massive presence can be fully felt as its undeviating position projects upward toward the sky. Its beauty represents an imposing posture that also aligns quite nicely with its form. Recognize how the toe shifted and moved away from its original positioning. It moved out of alignment with the other toes by moving inward. Over time, it might become a painful situation, but it need not be.

Know when doing this or other work, you may find another creation in nature more suitable. It is fine to move your focus from one thing to the next. Simply shift your focus to what you feel would better represent, to resolve, your specific issue. The key here is to visualize what you want to occur. Garner its attributes energetically and incorporate them into the dynamics of your desire. You are aligning with those preferred similarities and melding their characteristics into where you seek to enlist change.

In this example, one would perhaps not choose a weeping willow tree since it bends and curves. It might not be the best choice unless your preference is otherwise. Ask for the big toe to align and heal, remembering to qualify each request. Maintain your focus on this thing of beauty and wholeness in nature. See this as a most integral component. Look upon and resonate with this beautiful image as you blend it into your imaginings. Each time any straight, upward reaching tree is viewed or conceptualized, visualize and mentally see this toe moving to align with it. Then each time the big toe is seen, immediately envision and superimpose the massive tree upon it. See both aligned as one, together.

As you move to practice, make those choices which resonate with you. Now, what might you seek to practice upon as you play in the wonderment of it?

Take photos of your imaginings. Perhaps take time to travel, if not nearby, to a park or national forest. Go and see where the wonderful workings of nature reside. Each time you step into nature, allow a reset to be experienced. Can you feel a release occur when you go to the park, when you dig your toes into a sandy beach, or walk among the trees in the forest? Recognize the calming factor that is present there, as this break in your routine is an excellent way to de-stress from your daily activities. When you reconnect with nature, it can reset and recalibrate you. You see, nature was intended for that purpose — so connect and reconnect there often.

Do you understand how this works? Maybe that part of it would be helpful to know too. You see, as you focus on something, you draw it into your awareness. As you focus and do so from the perspective of amplifying key components, you again draw those aspects closer to you. So if you are wanting straighter toes, you focus on those representations within nature that allow a connection from a synergistic perspective to occur. As a co-creator, you have the right to formulate a world of your choosing. In a moment we will discuss the mystical component here. But first we want to make sure you understand the distinction in this discussion, so you are able to try this little exercise out for yourself.

In doing this work, you will find, too, that looking at what you want to manifest to be most helpful. So in this example, flip through a magazine or go onto the computer to view a perfectly placed toe or whatever it is you seek to change. Then see perfectly placed toes, as you visualize this throughout the day. As you now play in the field of possibility.

Continuing with the toe premise, perhaps you wonder why the toe moved inward initially. Maybe it is only in the formation stages of a bunion; maybe it is something else. But why has it moved out of alignment? This then goes back to the work we discussed earlier regarding trapped emotions. But one might say, *There is no pain with the toe. It's simply changing its position.* Before it moves into a more painful reality, seek its correction. Chart a new course before advancements occur. Let us look at why the toe is moving and determine the core issue at play. Reflect upon the past and find its correlation. What might have caused a misstep, or to be out of step, and what would allow for a redirection of steps taken? In other words, what would move one back in step if alignment is sought?

Do you see when doing this work, a somewhat contemplative or whimsical mode must be engaged to engage with the answers you seek? Work from that space and then seek answers. These are keys to unlock self-discoveries. Now you realize this little inconvenience is meant to be a guidepost and a means to set you back on course. It's important for you to recognize what's amiss. Without this answer, the course correction you seek may not come to pass. If it corrects and the situation recreates itself, then you have not yet discovered the core issue underfoot.

In order for these methods to work for you, reflect upon what you find. Yes, it may sound strange to say this is given as a measure of love, but it is so. You originally set up certain things you wanted to experience during this lifetime. How would you know you were adrift without being given some indication to course correct? Perhaps there are other preferred methods that will return you to your path. Those may be considered later, but for now, this is what is in play. So consider each sign as a gift. If you can see the benefit and give gratitude even when you do not fully understand what is being offered, then you will move into a different space within the Loving expanse and opportunity such insights offer.

Is there anything more that can be said to this point? Remember that Universe seeks to assist and provide you with all you desire. This is very important to remember and harder still to sometimes believe. You see, when the mind takes control, it is most cunning. At times, it can engage you without even being noticed. So become a good steward of what is going on there. To catch it at its own game is most entertaining. When you can get to that level of play, to outwit the wit is most fun. So watch and wait.

Observe the mental banter at play, and then shift your thoughts to a more preferred topic. Remove judgment of yourself and others in the process. This will allow better thoughts to take hold. Perhaps also seek to redirect your thoughts when some errant or rogue idea slips in. But know you are the ultimate gatekeeper of all that exists in your mental dialog. So if you recognize mental chatter that is not in keeping with your preference, feels bad, is not something you desire to engage with or draw to you, just change it. Remember, you have the ability to control your focus when you remain conscious of what is playing in your mind.

Know, too, you are not your thoughts. Your thoughts are separate from you. That might sound funny to imagine that you are not your thoughts, but this is so. Do not judge yourself in relation to your thoughts. Oftentimes, they float in and out without a full recognition of the intent or the content of their incessant banter. But do become conscious of what is transpiring and the tone of the dialog. Your mood will shift and you will be in higher spirits if you no longer engage in the negative thoughts you believe to be your own. Don't be embarrassed by those thoughts and don't judge them. Just shift to ones that make you feel happier and ones you enjoy thinking about.

You have set in motion each experience that presents itself back to you. See the benefit and the beauty of all that awaits you. In doing so, you will play out each potential drama postured from a better vantage. Accept and welcome what is, rather than pushing against your current reality. Implement new steps to administer the change you seek. Embrace what occurs in each and every situation, and you will move through these occurrences with greater ease. If you can also find gratitude, this, too, will in effect, move you into a better mental space.

As we move forward with this book and onto the next, we will look toward health and healing — how you might engage a change to occur in your atoms and allow them to recalibrate. These chapters are provided to allow you to engage varied understandings. Perhaps to understand one component, but not yet another. And so, now let us continue on together.

Let's look at the way your body functions. Does it fire at all levels? Is it as efficient for you as it was ten or twenty years ago? Do you wish you'd taken different steps in your past so you could still participate in activities enjoyed in your youth? Knowing that your purpose is not a thing but a vibration, how can you resonate at a certain vibrational level to do the thing you love, if you have discomfort or pain? If your gift is actually the vibration emanated by your being when engaged in activities you enjoy, can the intended frequency be generated while on pain medications?

You can overcome anything you set your mind to accomplish. Believe this from every pore in your body, down to your very core. Have you ever believed in anything to this extent before? You must know it with conviction; otherwise, it cannot be accomplished through the methods we describe. This must be fully accepted, understood, and embraced. So we will recommend for you to believe first, before continuing on.

It is in your total acceptance in the here and now that allows Universe to step in and assist to make your belief so. We know this may sound like folly, but this understanding is necessary to engage the process we will share. Can you resonate with these words? Not just read them, for many can read, but are you able to assimilate to employ what is said? Can you cast your doubts to the wind and believe, just this moment, this day?

It is from your belief of what might be that your new reality is determined. In this moment, you are your beliefs in all that you do and say for anything less than this is a denial of self. You can mask your core beliefs, but then in that false face, whom do you serve? Do you see the push/pull momentum created here? Recognize no true benefit exists from this line of thinking.

Let us move toward the understanding of atoms. Yes, atoms can be realigned to exist in a more exacting formation. Through your thoughts, you can redefine your world so that you may get about your business to be all that you intend. Perhaps a course correction is needed. Move from this awareness into acknowledgment. Bless and give gratitude for such understandings and then shift into this preferred reality — one that is more aligned with your renewed objectives and current intentions.

So let us continue to discuss the rotation of the atom. Its rotational spin sets into motion the universe within your system. When illness or other distortions enter into its sphere, imbalances and disruptive patterns develop within the rotation. As such, it creates an inharmonious revolution, as more is gathered and returned to you. Through right thinking, a realignment of these cells can occur, setting them on a more productive course. You see, all the tools you need to do this work are within you.

Continue to enlist medical counsel, but also play with this methodology as you shift your thoughts to hold those more preferred. Here your intent is to shift those aspects not in alignment and to have them consciously flow in a more preferred manner. In this way, these other aspects begin to shift and change to mirror that instead of this. They realign to flow in a more harmonious pattern … as you set the intention to have them flow in unison within the more preferred vibrational mix. So how might this best occur?

When we talk about an atom's rotational spin, we are referencing its normal existence, as its movement is critical to maintaining balance and symmetry in your life. Here there is much reliance on the body communicating from one system to the next. Each system has certain fundamental elements. So when they do not function in the manner expected, if they veer off-course and maintain a different rhythm, then their symmetry is off as well. They become altered when trying to align with another pattern. So when the new pattern introduced is not harmonious with the others, then all therein seek to shift and mirror that. You see, harmony and the resulting flow are each important here. So when you get sick, do doctors ask what's been going on in your life? Do they ask if you've had some emotional disturbance or provide something other than a diagnosis of symptoms, which were created as a result of what? You see, altered patterns are the what and symptoms develop as a result of the irregularities produced by an erratic rotational spin.

If you were born a certain way, and if it is not through a series of thoughts that these imbalances exist or resulting from a series of choices made previously, what then? When you enter life with various birth defects, how can anything be traced back to any life occurrence when this is how you arrived? Would it be unfair to say that you arrived with all the tools you need even when this appears to not be so? Why would someone seek to experience life in a way other than as you prefer? You perhaps would not choose this for your life, would another? Or is there yet another purpose? Yet, you chose to experience this and they to that and, well, would another choose your experience?

We cannot explain why some chose what they seek to experience in this day, what they want from their life situation, or what they want to feel while here on this planet. However, we do know it is their unique privilege to do so. It is their right to choose to feel and to fully embrace whatever they seek to discover. Did you seek a certain experience that necessitated yet another to engage in its premise? Sometimes another is needed so that your life experience might be fully realized. And too, others are enlisted to help with your journey to experience and complete what could not be realized without them.

And perhaps you would say, *Well, I would not choose this for myself. I would not choose this current experience.* And we would respond that you may not have chosen the precise circumstance in which you now reside, but it resulted from previous choices made. And it will get you to your next step, where you might go, in order to do and be. Do you see? Each experience is a stepping stone for the next. Can you then give gratitude and thank Universe for giving you direction and guidance? In this way, you can see where you are on your path. Now you know you are in step as you are directed toward the next one. Can you do this?

If someone promotes angst within your life, if they stir you up like no other, understand their role. When they know how to push your buttons, can you now see how they offer you insights and vistas not seen before? This energetic connection has enabled you to find what was not evident earlier. There is an emotional trigger buried so deeply within, you didn't even know it was there. Wow, what a gift. Do you see this? Can you think on all of this a bit differently now? Once you recognize what these ones came to provide, they will no longer have the same impact upon you. With this one realization, can you see more clearly the energetic link which they alone can activate due to their uniquely held connection?

And too, if a drama has continued on in your life for what seems like a long time, do not be perplexed. Time does not exist as you believe, and so what seems like an eternity is but a flash of light. Time is short here on this planet, and one's life span is as a mere moment. So cherish each moment as you walk your days here.

Returning now to the rotational spin of the atom, recognize how it moves in sequence to keep your body operating harmoniously. Can you set an intention to remove something now that needs clearing out? Once you recognize the value of pain, discomfort, illness, and the like, they will no longer exist as you formerly believed. There is value in each step you have taken and even those you perceived earlier to be a misstep. All is not as you once understood. You see, as you move down the road, it eventually connects to another route that will take you closer to where you want to be. And so each step is of value and merit.

If you sought to shift and release a condition that was no longer necessary or of service to you, seeing each thing as being beneficial as you give gratitude for it, what might you choose to focus upon now? Might you recalibrate your cells to bring them back into a more aligned state and to be out-pictured as they once were? We believe this to be your best option and recognize in order for any shift to occur, it must also resonate as being plausible.

YOU MUST BELIEVE FIRST

If you believe this to be impossible, then, of course, it is and will be impossible for you to manifest such a change. But if you were to believe, just today, what would you need to know to allow for such a shift to be experienced? What might you need to do, beyond belief, to change any current condition?

Rotation is a word that is often misunderstood. What is rotation but a surge of energetic components that allow for shifts to occur. What is meant by this? Energy is quite simply a series of pulsations that result in a spin of sorts when considering the atom and other molecular components. As these spins occur, there is a sequence or symmetry to their internal workings, for they correspond and respond to the energy emitted. In the harmony that existed there before, your body operated in a most seamless manner.

When the symmetry you had known before became altered through the introduction of certain new elements, their balance and flow were disrupted. Their symmetry was no more. Now what had operated most effortlessly met with resistance. This resistance did not formerly exist. And so, the flow and its earlier pattern became altered. In so much as this caused everything in and around that area to become disjointed and out of alignment with the congruency it had known when a newly introduced pattern emerged. This new pattern corresponded differently. It truly was no longer engaged in the harmonious rhythm it had once known, but rather it became a mismatched, incongruent series of pulsations that impacted its rotational spin. When this newly introduced energy was in its formation stages, it sought integration and incorporation with the other. Thus, the harmonious rhythm known before was sought again. Now the objective became to align differently to restore balance.

RECLAIM WHAT WAS AND IS MORE PREFERRED
WHEN YOU MAINTAIN BETTER THOUGHTS

Shifting to maintain positive thoughts buoys up your energy. Your vibration will shift to mirror your newly aligned focus. Attune the body as you seek its perfection as you engage to restore it to a more aligned state and back to its original design. Find the preferred flow, rather than aligning to incongruent, disjointed patterns. These disrupt and interrupt the harmonious energy once engaged.

Do you know why pain, disease, or some illness is present and now a part of your life? If you have done work throughout the process of reading this book, you are aware of some of the components at play. Do you see the beauty in what you experience? For truly, mile markers provide guidance when they are recognized. If your outer and inner world are not in alignment, then how else would you know to regroup if you did not have some indicator to show you where you now reside?

Do you look at your life with awareness as a conscious participant rather than one who is caught within an ever-changing environment? If you are engaged and act in thoughtful consideration and make conscious choices, rather than reactionary ones, what alternate reality might you experience? Do you see this? Can you engage in life to see the varied opportunities that await your discovery rather than enlisting reactionary responses instead? Now you have more options from which to choose, and this allows better choices to come in and be experienced. Perhaps now you can see one with more appeal. One you didn't see before. As you sit and ponder all of this, decide today to be open to something new ... something that will bridge what you knew yesterday with something new today.

Heal, Restore, Renew

Now let's begin an exercise of renewal and rejuvenation. As you breathe in, feel the air circulate through your airways and throughout your body. Recognize the feeling of this air fluidly flowing within you. Imagine this to be the purest elixir that exists on this planet. Feel the difference and the benefits this rejuvenating prana provides to your system. Breathe in this limitless supply of infused, specially calibrated oxygen. This is how you might add to the understanding you held on Light Energy as this is the purest, specially charged elixir known to exist. It has been created expressly for you. It renews and refreshes your entire body. See it course throughout your system and saturate each part of you. Focus now as it fully rejuvenates each organ, airway, and component within your form. It has many uses, and the formula devised is unique unto you.

Now focus like a laser beam on those smaller aspects such as cells within your body. See all move together in symmetry and purpose, like miniature galaxies that vibrate in sequence. See them move in the beauty and grace in which they were designed. Do not focus or concentrate on those things that are in need of a boost, but rather see instead their progression into a state of health and vitality. See these healthy cells as they recalibrate and move as other healthy cells do. Express and feel gratitude. Feel Love and appreciation as a renewed vibrancy streams through all parts of your body. Allow for the body's total and complete healing, its absolute perfection to formulate. Do not acknowledge any pain or any other shortcoming, only what you want to draw into your immediate reality as you manifest a new blueprint into this world of form.

Can you see the beauty of your body and how it serves you? Do you thank Universe, God, or whomever you recognize as the Deity Essence that oversees all? Do you acknowledge your connection to that Essence as being another extension of Source Energy here on Earth? Will you allow this Essence to infuse your body temple with its main component, Love? Do you remember the definition of Universal Love discussed earlier?

Now might you feel this Love as it flows into your being in the form of the pure oxygenated elixir we have described? Blanket your entire being with this special elixir as you visualize it inside, outside, and all about you. As you merge into a oneness with these things, become enveloped in this velvety substance. Feel its warmth against your skin emanate out as it serves to comfort and protect. Then breathe. Remember to breathe deeply and continuously throughout this process.

Feel each cell in your form invigorated by this pure oxygenated elixir as you are once again infused by it. As it courses throughout your form, a renewal starts as you are enveloped and wrapped in an energetic cocoon. Let your former self relinquish its hold on this day as it retreats back to the past.

Look for a renewed form to emerge from this space. Recognize protection exists during the healing process as this sheath overlays your physical form. Feel comfort and the essence of Love, which swirls about you now. It provides support and a stabilizing quality as you visualize it extending three feet beyond you in all directions. Ruby in color, this energy lightly pulsates in unison with your heart.

Visualize this as you enter into a short meditation. Still the mind, as you allow its energetic formation to occur. It is not unusual to feel heat flowing from your body at this time. Meditate to reinforce these steps as you reflect upon the following verse.

Healing Light so bright and bold,
your wondrous gift I now behold.
Bless me now to my delight,
as all aligns to be made right.

Focus now as a laser beam upon the area that seeks recharge. The ruby cocoon, although transparent by design, has superior strength in its healing qualities. You can see your body in all its perfection through its energetic, translucent covering as you focus upon these areas, which now begin to align and restore in their shift. Do you see how you can more easily move about after having called it into action? It can be engaged without imposing any limitation during its activation.

Continue to re-engage it by visualizing it around your form. If you prefer a modification, see a smaller version around a more specific area. It is important to engage this matrix around your entire form first before you seek to minimize or localize it. Then you can place it around a more modified area in need of repair.

Upon your repeated visualization, you engage and re-engage its action and its unique capabilities as they are directed toward the area of interest. See the ruby cocoon intensify as it restores balance to your entire body and then to the preferred location. Employ deep breathing throughout this time. Cup your hands in front of you as you visualize to create energy orbs to further infuse restorative energy during this process. Move this energy within and into those areas needing a renewal or boost after its formation.

Now engage a most specific matrix into action as you recite the passages which follow. The matrix of Love has been a healing medium in past times and is now reactivated for your use in this day. Feel the wonderment of it as you experience the limitless potential which does now exist. Draw forth unbounded renewal energy as you move this matrix into action this day. Create and direct inwardly to recharge and rebalance what existed before. Fill energy voids and openings as they now become infused, aligned and restored.

Universal Love Matrix

Healing Light so bright and bold
this gift of Love I now behold.
Strengthen, align to now make right
    what was hidden from Earthly sight.
I enlist to ignite all that might be
    as body restoration is essential and key.

Wholeness realigned within me will stay
    as Universal Love is purposely called into play.
Love flows in and through to redirect
    what was amiss and hard to detect.
This harmonious energy integrates once more
    as stagnation and pain are removed to their core.

This recalibration aligns, removes, transcends,
    deletes, retards, what's fettered within.
When Light and Love are called into play,
    Universal Love rushes in to clear away
    all limitation of body and mind,
    invoked once again to shift all of its kind.

Healing Light so bright and bold
    your wondrous gift I now behold.
Bless me now through Love made Light,
    as all is transformed through
    Healing — Energetic — Light.

In this action, you set into motion the recalibration and rotational spin of an atom. That which rotated in an erratic manner before now moves to shift its rotation to become more aligned in its renewal. We tell you all is possible when you believe you can enact such change into your being and world. Belief is a powerful thing. And so, do see if this work resonates with you.

If you are able to cast away old paradigms of thought to allow for more transitory, uplifting thoughts of change and possibility to exist, then you can potentially rewrite your current script. Yet if you prefer the current play in progress, your life can remain in its status quo scenario. You must want a new script to enlist change to occur in your life. Unlimited opportunities await you, but they originate from a space of belief of what might be. And when you believe that another reality can be yours, then it can be so.

The mind is a sticky and tricky thing to get around. So we advise you to get the reins of control back so you can evoke the change you were meant to create. Then claim all that is yours awaiting manifestation. Should you continue to allow the mind or ego to run rampant within, then desired changes will be more difficult to accomplish.

As you move into other areas of discussion beyond this book, please refer back to these pages as you continue to expand your vibration while incorporating other avenues of healing into the mix of your activities. As you seek to implement the teachings gathered from these pages, know there are no missteps. We have said this before and ask you to not give up if you try one method one time without getting the immediate result you seek. Do not leave discouraged if you have not quickly connected to the endeavors you desire to manifest.

Know that depending on your level of engagement with these words, you may need to employ a bit of practice to get and keep the flow engaged. As you consider other methods, know all aligns according to your intentioned focus and belief. In this way, you shift from *what if* thinking to embrace *what is* as you seek more. We hope you find each measure introduced here intriguing and beneficial. Do not hold out for something in the future, but practice the steps provided to allow for change to enter into your current reality.

All of Heaven and Earth are behind your every success. So we say this is not our last encounter as we look to bring forward additional teachings. The momentum you develop in the process will make a lasting difference to your continued health and the quality of your life for years to come.

Go in Love, Be in Love
and
Connect with Us
Always through Love.

And so it is.

About the Elders

Think upon Us as a Consciousness of Light and Love. Think upon Us as ever-moving Light that does fluctuate and form words within the in-breath and out-breath of a beat or measure. Think upon Us as Love, in Love with all that is.

We are Love from the Consciousness of Love. We are known as those who were and are considered the Elders. This is a name that was devised a time or two ago by those who sought such knowledge according to their lineage and birth. We kept this title as it was more recently devised than others that could also have been used.

We are Beings that wish for humanity to have answers that have eluded them in recent times. There are those who have shared such information, but it is also being released in this manner, in this time, so there might be a profound knowingness as one engages with life here.

We are Pure Consciousness. We are many, and We provide insights for humanity so that more might be gleaned in this lifetime than without such knowledge. We are Love, but all are that which is.

About the Author

Robyn G. Locke bridges the physical with the nonphysical world to bring you purpose-driven, self-healing, self-help books. She is a transformation facilitator, international speaker, energy intuitive, and spiritual seeker.

Love life. Even what appears to be bad. Discover the deeper meaning attached to each thing encountered along the way. Engage in life's mystery in this way.

These inspirational writings are given by the Elders. They provide invaluable insights and suggest refreshingly simple steps to engage. Imagine your future when mental constructs are removed and replaced with purposeful direction. Unbounded opportunities await as you consciously co-create all you desire to manifest.

About Our Books

The Greater Purpose
Awaken to Your Reason for Being

The Greater Purpose **works in tandem with**
Awaken: The Definitive Guide to Transformative Change

Ready to reach your full potential in this life journey?
Tap into who you are and what you are meant to discover
in this rediscovery of a lifetime.

Are you searching for answers to address your greater purpose and why you are here? You know you are more than you can see and touch, so is it time to put into motion some subtleties you don't yet know? Are you ready? Tap into that spiritual part of you and what you are meant to uncover in this pivotal discovery. International speaker, transformation facilitator, and energy intuitive Robyn G. Locke bridges the physical to the non-physical world to convey insights from the Elders — Beings of Pure Consciousness and Infinite Awareness. Their unlimited and unbounded perspectives are given in unconditional Love while shining a Light on Universal Love and its many purposeful pathways.

Their non-judgmental and uniquely held authority suggests how you might awaken to enact all you are in search of. Whether that means self-realization or procuring the best and most bountiful life. Your unimaginable future waits in readiness. Lay claim to your unique gifts as you unearth this ultimate means of personal transformation.

Are you in the doings of your purpose, yet await true fulfillment and the means to move manifestations into motion? Are you routinely and consciously seeking more? If you're ready for small shifts that will result in epic proportions, look no further.

The Greater Purpose is a series of guiding truths and the definitive means of determining and living that original intent. Awaken to the inspiration of your mission through the many nuances you'll explore. Delve into foundational and fundamental understandings as you remove mental limitations and their constructs. Now move to ascertain what you sought to know once long ago. Grow heart-centered awareness and intuition as you connect the dots to this formula for inner fulfillment. You'll see life and all within it differently as your vibration shifts accordingly. *The Greater Purpose* is made up of the purpose trilogy. Within this book series, you'll find —

BOOK ONE: *The Little Book to Find Your Purpose*
- The expansiveness of Universal Love and its transformative measures
- Steps to still and slow the mind as you understand why you are not your thoughts

BOOK TWO: *The Original Purpose*
- The steps to recognize and enact your original purpose
- Answers to the age-old question, *Why am I here?*

BOOK THREE: *Enact Your Purpose*
- Energetic keys to elevate your frequency and help you unlock the underlying premise of your purpose
- Effective ways to enact change as you implement some simple steps that will transform your existence and revolutionize how you see this life, and much, much more

Are you searching for answers to address your greater purpose and why you are here? If you are looking for life-changing perceptions, an easy way to integrate knowledge the mind can't conjecture, along with energy keys to Universal Love and what it enables, then step into another portal of possibility as you engage all-encompassing, timeless wisdoms of the ages.

Your roadmap to success, good health, and happiness
as you consciously co-create all you desire.

Given in Love
How to Make This Your Last Incarnation

Ready to understand why you are here and make this the last incarnation?

Discover the pathway beyond living life here
as you become consciously aware and
your purpose-driven objectives become realized.

Do you desire to extend beyond your thoughts and current mental limitations? Do you understand the benefit of focusing on your heart? Want to break the endless cycle of incarnating yet again? International speaker, transformation facilitator, and energy intuitive, Robyn G. Locke holds the energetic key to connect to the Elders, vis-à-vis her Soul. Her Soul is a part of their community. These Beings seek to share in an unlimited way, so you might find your pathway beyond living life here. As a part of the Elder Community, Robyn's Soul came to remind humanity of their divinity, and why they chose to embody.

Given in Love is the means to finding your inner fulfillment, while removing self-limiting self-talk. Replace negative thoughts that cause depression, anxiety, addiction, and mental fatigue with better-feeling thoughts. Move the mind out of the way to reconnect with your deeply held divinity. When you tap into that inner truth, discover more than you might now imagine. Detach, unleash, and satisfy the Agreement as you move beyond this *Earth Experience*. Transform and restore wholeness once again.

In *Given in Love*, you'll discover —

- How to enact life with intention and the steps that will enable this to be your last incarnation.
- Ways to access a consciously aware existence that taps into the heart space.
- Your one true ambition and the purpose you sought to know.
- The means to align with that highly attuned part of you — your Spiritual Essence.

- Locate new avenues to transform, shift, and change. Discover new understandings as they surface from deep within, as your perspectives shift and new opportunities come into view.

Given in Love is a powerful guide. Its many truths are not known currently. Unearth rare wisdom and guidance chronicled within the many insights found here, and given in the Love meant to nourish both your heart and Soul. If you like profound enlightenment, straightforward advice, and resolutions enabled by the mysteries of your past, then you'll be inspired by Robyn G. Locke and the Elders' remarkable teachings. Discover now what you did not know before. For how can you truly know until you do?

**Enact steps found within *Given in Love*
to reclaim what has been lost over time!**

Connect with Us

Find us at

https://AdvancedEnergetics.org

www.Facebook.com/AdvancedEnergetics

www.Instagram.com/AdvancedEnergetics

www.YouTube.com/AdvancedEnergetics

www.ingramcontent.com/pod-product-compliance
Lightning Source LLC
Chambersburg PA
CBHW071145130626
46553CB00004B/1528